RUNNING TO THE

IMPOSSIBLE

by

MARIOS ELLINAS

DEDICATION

I dedicate this book to Danielle—my wonderful wife, my best friend, and my greatest source of encouragement.

....and to Christos, Caleb, and Chloe—the coolest kids on Planet Earth! You inspire me and keep me dreaming. There is no limit to what God will do in you and through you. I love you!

ACKNOWLEDGEMENTS

I offer thanks to my parents, Andreas and Irene Ellinas for giving me a great upbringing and for always upholding and modeling the great virtues of love, integrity, faithfulness, and diligence. I thank them for being such wonderful motivators and encouragers in my life!

I thank Nancy Shariff for transcribing my message series, *Running to the Impossible*. I would have never been able to write this book without her assistance and support.

A huge I LOVE YOU to all my brothers and sisters in Christ at *Valley Shore Assembly of God*. This book is a product of their great courage and faith in the face of impossibilities.

I am eternally grateful to Rev. C. Ronald Bradley for leading me to Christ, pouring his life in me, and teaching me by example the supreme commandment, love.

I bow my heart with thanks to Rev. and Mrs. W. Dwayne Harper for loving me, mentoring me, and giving me the opportunity to serve in God's Kingdom.

I am grateful to Jason Westerfield for his friendship and support. I thank him for his willingness to contribute the Foreword.

I salute all my friends who read the book and offered their insightful feedback and endorsements. I love and appreciate them!

Many thanks to Peter Sylvester for his assistance with the formatting of the manuscript.

A big thank you to my friend, Kathy Hartley, for undertaking the monumental task of editing this book. I especially thank her for being so gracious, patient, and kind with areas that needed correction or improvement.

ENDORSEMENTS

Spend any kind of time with Marios Ellinas and you will immediately encounter a frontline leader in this generation who hungers for the God of the impossible to reveal Himself in everyday situations. The message that flows from Marios' heart is that of contending relentlessly to know God more intimately, which results in God's Spirit flowing through him in greater measure. As he delivers this proclamation of running *to* and *through* the impossible, it flows from a vessel that is filled with the integrity of this revelation and from a heart that is surrendered to the purposes of God. This message matches the messenger. Marios is leading a culture of people who are becoming more comfortable with the "uncomfortable," the situations that push us into greater realms of faith, thus allowing for God to do above all we could ever imagine.

Mark DeJesus
Founder – Turning Hearts Ministries

Looking for excitement, courage, and motivation? Then simply pick up this masterpiece that has been penned by one of God's up and coming generals. Pastor Marios has been living this title "Running to the Impossible" in his daily walk with God. Spend any time with the author and you will be fused with a sense of urgency to go on a deeper journey with the Spirit of God. As you read this work you will quickly recognize the desire of the writer to help each believer understand that "Greater is He who is within thee," than anything that could ever come against us. Every student, author, teacher, minister, and five-fold ministry gift will be stirred after reading this inspiring work. Enjoy your pursuit.

Pastor Reginald Stewart
International Family Worship Center

In God's eyes, now is the time for great dreams and large visions. Thankfully, passing away are the days of mediocre men and limited thinking. Pastor Marios Ellinas declares with boldness and spiritual authority, the great dream God has for His people, and the great people God has in His dream. A prophetic must read message to all God's people!

Erik A. Kudlis, President and CEO, Erik's Design Build Associates, Inc.

It's been said that a man with fear dies a thousand deaths every day, but the man with courage, dies just once. Marios Ellinas is a man with great courage. *Running to the Impossible* was written out of a living testimony of perseverance and faith. Many times during the reading I would stop to *listen* to the words written on the page before me. Marios has revealed treasures from Scripture to bring clarity and skill for overcoming the impossibilities of life. *Running to the Impossible* is a "NOW" book, relevant, wisdom-filled, and prayerfully written. If you know that God has a calling on your life but lack the courage to walk it out, this is a *must* read.

Gina Blaze
New England Prayer Center

We live in a dream-stealing world where our hopes and dreams are put on trial through the eyes of men. We are constantly told what we can or cannot accomplish, what is possible and what is not. In this phenomenal book, Pastor Marios will motivate and equip you with the Truth about your own dreams and aspirations – that *all* things from God are possible for those who believe. He will inspire and encourage you that faith will replace your fear when you simply take that first step toward running to your "impossible". And then...watch for what God does in your life!

J.D. Porcelli
Entrepreneur

As I was reading a copy of "Running to the Impossible", I began to think about when I met Marios fifteen years ago. All the time I have known him, I have found him to be a man hungry for God. This book demonstrates how through determination we can accomplish the dreams and visions God puts on our hearts. Marios is a man with "iron in his soul". This is his story; he has lived it. If he can "Run to the Impossible," so can you!

Doug Eccles
Holy Ghost Celebration Ministries

Table of Contents

FOREWORD

"Running to the Impossible" is a hallmark tribute to God and what He can do through those who believe Him. This book by Marios Ellinas will capture your heart's passion to confront impossibilities head on, and it will stir your faith to achieve greater things than you have ever imagined.

Marios has done a magnificent job in taking the classic epic battle of David and Goliath and making it a contemporary story we can all relate to. Any person reading "Running to the Impossible" will be challenged to persevere no matter what seemingly impossible difficulties come his/her way. Marios has very graphically portrayed step by step what King David, and you and I, deal with when impossibilities are in front of us. He has also shown us how to properly handle these situations with wisdom, so we can finish with success.

Every person will face impossibilities. The question remains, "How will we respond?" If we respond correctly we will see God's power work on our behalf, and we will experience the benefits and rewards for faith and a courageous heart.

This book will challenge your fears, and push you to the faith and boldness that lead to greatness despite the odds. There is nothing impossible with God, and Marios has shown us that there is nothing impossible for us when we walk with God. The same God that worked for King David to defeat Goliath is the same supernatural God working on our behalf.

I have had the greatest pleasure of knowing and walking through life with Marios and Danielle Ellinas. I marvel at how this isn't just a book Marios has written, but it is an invitation and a window that peers into the Ellinas' life story. They have continually prayed and believed God for the impossible, despite the size of the giants they were facing.

I have watched how God has always come through for them. I have also personally witnessed supernatural miracles take place through their lives as they trust God to deliver, heal, protect, and provide for other people. Their prayers get through to heaven and have results. This couple runs to the impossible with great tenacity of faith and boldness, exemplifying courage to the rest of us, while at the same time revealing true humility, love, and sincerity of heart toward others. True love gives generously; true love is courageous and brave. I have had the delight to witness these virtues so eloquently presented in their lives.

We must believe, not back down, and run full speed into our walls of resistance; and we must do so until we break through. This book will stir you up to the point where you can't sit back any more and tolerate the giants in your life. After reading it, you too will be motivated to conquer impossibilities and walk in victory. One thing that is impossible is to read this book and not get an impartation of God's Spirit of courage!

Jason T. Westerfield

Founder and President

Kingdom Reality Ministries

www.kingdomreality.com

INTRODUCTION

My first memorable confrontation against the impossible occurred in the summer of 1988. I grew up on the island of Cyprus. At the age of eighteen, every Cypriot male serves his country through mandatory military conscription. From a young age, knowing that one day I too would be a soldier, I aspired to join the most renowned and best-trained branch of the army, the Green Berets.

I kept my dream to myself for many years, but during my freshman year in high school, I began to share it with friends and family. With the exception of my parents, who always believed in me and encouraged me, everyone who heard of my plans responded, *"Impossible!"*

In their eyes, I was too thin, too weak, too sensitive and too tender-hearted to survive Green Beret boot camp and endure the rigors of Special Forces life. Moreover, hundreds of individuals tried out for the Green Berets every year. More than half would fail the fitness test, and only a few hundred would be picked from those who passed.

"You, a Green Beret? Impossible!" they said.

Determined to live my dream and prove my critics wrong, I joined a track team, participated in team sports, and trained with weights for three years. I developed relationships with several former Green Berets and asked them hundreds of questions. I read books and watched films about Green Berets. I simply did my best to prepare physically and emotionally for Special Forces training.

In June of 1988, only a few days after graduating high school, I enlisted in the Cyprus armed forces. I signed up for the Green Berets and lined up for the ominous fitness test.

Along with multiple other hopefuls, I ran laps, did push-ups and pull-ups, and performed various drills. In every area of testing I ranked in the top three. Several Green Beret drill sergeants had looked my way favorably; some had even made positive comments about my performance. At the end of the fitness test, I was confident I would be chosen!

The next day around noontime, the barracks loudspeakers came to life with the names of the recruits who had been selected for Green Beret training. Many names were called, but mine was not one of them.

I was devastated. My life-dream was slipping away. For years I had heard the word "impossible" regarding my ambition. Through research, training, and the preparation of my heart and body, I had managed to block out those negative voices and had kept my dream alive. But in that moment, when it was obvious I had not been picked, a door seemed to have shut on me with a thud of finality. On that door hung a sign saying, "Impossible. Especially for YOU — Do not enter!"

I watched as one comrade after another packed his belongings and headed towards the transport trucks for Green Beret boot camp. Rejection and limitation screamed at me, *"Too skinny! Too weak! The officers saw right through you. They knew you didn't have it in you."*

When the last man had boarded the bus and the doors shut, a renewed resolve arose in me, which I will never forget.

I gritted my teeth and spoke the words, *"It's not over!"*

I found a friend from my school who had also done well on the fitness test, but had likewise not been selected. I informed him of my plan, and together we marched across a large soccer field to the officers' clubhouse. We knocked on the door, and when a young soldier answered, we stated the purpose for our "visit."

"We want to speak with the highest ranking Green Beret officer, right now. We have an urgent message for him."

The soldier told us to wait outside. After a few minutes, an imposing Green Beret major came out. With his stature, his physical appearance, his demeanor, and even his voice, the officer standing before us personified everything I had expected to find in a Green Beret.

He walked right up to us, got in our faces, and demanded an explanation. Not only had we disturbed his afternoon rest, we had also broken the chain of command by going directly to a high-ranking officer such as himself.

With penetrating eyes, formidable posture, and great authority, he asked, *"What on earth do you want?"* (I'm paraphrasing a bit.)

My friend spoke first. He told the major that we strongly desired to be Green Berets, we felt we had been wronged during the selection process, and consequently, we had resolved to escape from the barracks that night so we could hitchhike our way to the Green Beret training camp.

"We will find our way to your unit, Sir," my friend contended, "and we will wait outside until you take us in and train us."

First the Major grinned, then he laughed, and finally he frowned. He moved so close to us that his face was only inches away. In the most intimidating tone of voice, he said:

"You go AWOL (Absent Without Official Leave) from this place, and you'll be arrested, court-martialed, and most likely serve time in jail. Now get out of my face, and get back to your company." With that stern warning, he turned away and walked towards the clubhouse.

Before I had time to process it, before I could even think it through, it happened:

"I don't think you understand, Sir!" I yelled at the top of my lungs.

"We *will* jump this wall tonight, and you *may* arrest us, and you *may* court-martial us, and the government *may* throw us in jail, but when our time is served, Sir, we will find our way to the Green Beret training camp and wait outside until you take us in and train us. I don't think you understand just how badly we want this…Sir!"

The officer turned around, fixed his eyes on me, and looked me up and down for what seemed an eternity. Then he spoke in a shockingly calm tone.

"If I could train five men with your kind of heart, surely we would prevail over any enemy."

That evening my friend and I were on a transport vehicle, heading to Green Beret boot camp with a personal commendation from the officer, who turned out to be a highly respected and very influential Green Beret!

During the long ride to the military base, I couldn't stop thinking about how my childhood dream was coming true. I would train with the best and be one of them. I would grow in physical strength and ability. I would proudly wear the Green Beret uniform. I would become a warrior. I had never been so ecstatic!

It took years to understand what had really transpired that day. Deep inside me something had shifted. I had gone toe to toe with an impossibility that had plagued me for years, and I had won. I had pushed aside fear and limitation, and I had conquered new territory!

In many ways, the incident outside the officers' clubhouse launched me into my destiny—not just as a warrior in the Cyprus Special Forces, but also as a soldier for the God of the Bible.

Having served in both armies, I have discovered that they are very different in multiple ways; however, there is one common quality that makes all the difference for survival and significance: a willingness to risk everything and run towards the impossible.

CHAPTER 1

THE IMPOSSIBLE

Impossibility is that which we cannot accomplish, resolve, or fulfill merely by applying our own natural ability, determination, understanding, or experience. It is the objective we cannot attain, the goal we cannot meet, and the fight we cannot win using the resources that are found within ourselves.

No one is exempt from impossibility; it is indiscriminate and unavoidable. Everyone at some point in life sets objectives, entertains dreams, and encounters challenges that are impossible.

It may be an A+ for a student who has always received C's and D's. It could be a spot in the starting lineup for the athlete who is repeatedly perceived as the team "benchwarmer." For some it is the promotion to the top ranks of the company; for others it is the acquisition of a certain vehicle or a first home. For the parent it may be the return of a wayward child; for the scientist, the breakthrough in her field; for the pastor, the growth of the church to one thousand in attendance; for the invalid, his restoration to full health.

The question for us should never be, "Will we encounter the impossible?" Rather, the question is, "How will we respond in that encounter?"

For an entrepreneur, it may seem impossible to obtain another one million dollars to launch a new multi-million dollar business. For a couple contemplating their child's first year of college tuition, impossibility may take the form of $30,000 added to the family's annual budget. The needs and numbers in these two cases are very different, yet there is one common denominator. Both face an impossible situation.

The question for us should never be, *"Will we encounter the impossible?"* Rather, the question is, *"How will we respond in that encounter?"*

Impossibility may be compared to a magnet. Magnets have the capacity both to repel and to attract, depending on the magnetic properties of the objects within their range. When most individuals face impossibilities, they are initially repelled.

No one enjoys pain or discomfort; therefore, we naturally shy away from potentially painful or uncomfortable experiences. Our natural response in the face of a seemingly insurmountable problem is to try and wrench ourselves free from it.

Over the last twelve years, I have been under-going annual laser treatments to remove a birth-mark from my face. Doctor Cyrus Chess of the Dermatological Center of Connecticut shoots tiny beams of laser through the skin on my face to de-stroy capillaries that lie too close to the surface.

The process is painful. Every few moments, the doctor has to remind me to turn my face back to-wards him, because without realizing it, I shun the pain-inflicting laser probe in his hand.

"We naturally pull away from noxious stimuli," Dr. Chess explains. It is true! No one likes pain, and no one likes impossibilities.

When confronted with the diagnosis of malig-nancy, the financial impasse, the hard-hearted loved one, or the enormous project on deck, our first thought is not *"Bring it on!"* Just as we would naturally pull away from the dentist's drill, the ill-tasting medicine or any other uncomfortable expe-rience, we try to avoid impossibility.

Because they flee the impossible, many people never enter their destiny. They contemplate a par-ticular breakthrough, pursuit, or dream for months, maybe years. They envision great results. They invest much time and many resources, but suddenly, they come up against an obstacle that seems insurmountable. Impossibility looms over them like a gigantic scarecrow and gets the best of them.

The college student meets the tough professor and his stringent course requirements. The minister is challenged by an ornery parishioner or board member. The parent hits a brick wall in trying to communicate with his children. The entrepreneur cannot seem to win the confidence of potential investors. The patient is not making progress in overcoming a debilitating disease. The recovering addict keeps stumbling and starting over from square one.

Regardless of the challenge at hand, everyone comes to the place where the price seems too high, the sacrifice too painful, the mountain too tall. Many give up at the very juncture that would offer the best opportunity for maturity, advancement, and blessing. They begin to focus their attention on less formidable tasks than impossibilities, and waste the chance to fulfill their dreams.

Impossibility has a significant role in our growth and maturity as individuals. Some of our greatest breakthroughs in life are attained when we choose to face impossibilities head-on.

There comes a point for those who know God, continually seek His will, and strive to live victoriously in Him, when they overcome their fear of the impossible through relationship with Christ and an understanding of God's Word. Instead of trying to circumvent mountains, they find the courage and strength to try to climb them, tunnel through them, or better yet, inspired by Mark

11:23, boldly speak to the mountains that they may be removed.

> *If anyone says to this mountain, "Go, throw yourself into the sea," and does not doubt in his heart but believes that what he says will happen, it will be done for him.*
> (Mark 11:23)

In other words, there comes a point when we have to face the impossibility, and instead of running *from* it, we must actually run *to* it, because there is great treasure to be obtained in the process, and eternal benefits for those who overcome.

Jesus said in Matthew 19:26, "*...with God all things are possible,*" and again in Mark 9:23, "*...all things are possible to him who believes.*" The apostle Paul, speaking in the context of being able to sustain himself both with little and with much, said in Philippians 4:13, "*I can do all things through Christ who strengthens me.*" Therefore, the believer in Jesus Christ is expected and even mandated, not just to face the impossible, but also to actually run towards it and conquer it, especially when it stands in the way of his or her purpose in life.

The process of taking on impossibilities is a catalyst for spiritual growth and life-changing breakthrough.

Running to the Impossible explores the process by which impossibility changes from being a repellant to a force of attraction. The chapters of this book provide a biblical context for us to understand and embrace the following truth:

The process of taking on impossibilities is a catalyst for spiritual growth and life-changing breakthrough.

When we stop seeing impossibility as a forbidding roadblock to our goals and dreams, but instead view it as our opportunity to grow in faith, love, and intimacy with God, we attain new levels of spiritual maturity. Confronting the impossible launches us into a process by which we recognize that every obstacle or challenge we choose to run towards, leads us to a fresh revelation of the person and nature of our Lord, Jesus Christ.

Moreover, we escape from the clutches of fear or limitation and run right into the loving arms of our Heavenly Father. Once we encounter the grace, protection, provision, and care that stem from God's love for us, we are changed forever.

The amazing benefits we receive throughout our journey, and especially the rewards on the other side of our "mountains," leave us, not only with a sense of accomplishment, but also with a desire for more of the same.

The concept of running to the impossible is well illustrated by a pivotal incident in the life of a young Jewish shepherd from Bethlehem. His name was David, and the impossibility before him was a Philistine super-warrior named Goliath.

CHAPTER 2

GIANT IN THE WAY!

The Philistines stood on a mountain on one side, and Israel stood on a mountain on the other side, with a valley between them. And a champion went out from the camp of the Philistines, named Goliath, from Gath, whose height was six cubits and a span. He had a bronze helmet on his head, and he was armed with a coat of mail, and the weight of the coat was five thousand shekels of bronze. And he had bronze armor on his legs and a bronze javelin between his shoulders. Now the staff of his spear was like a weaver's beam, and his iron spearhead weighed six hundred shekels; and a shield-bearer went before him.
(1 Samuel 17:3-7)

In the eyes of Israel's army, Goliath was more than a Philistine soldier, more than a seasoned fighter, more than an archenemy. He was the personification of impossibility.

Goliath was about nine feet tall. He had a body frame strong enough to bear a bronze helmet, a one-hundred and twenty-five pound coat of mail, bronze shin guards, bronze armor for his thighs, a sword in one hand, and a spear in the other. The spearhead alone weighed fifteen pounds! Imagine a warrior who was still fully agile despite being clad with the equivalent of a two hundred pound person on his back, and holding a twenty-five pound weapon in each hand!

For forty days, twice every day (1 Samuel 17:16), Goliath walked into the no-man's land between the two armies hurling threats, taunts, and insults against God's people on the other side. His formidable appearance was coupled with a language replete with intimidation and propaganda:

> *Then he stood and cried out to the armies of Israel, and said to them, "Why have you come out to line up for battle?"*
> (1 Samuel 17:8)

Have you ever heard it?

"Why do you even bother applying for that job? You're not good enough. You're not qualified! Others have better credentials than you."

"Why do you bother studying for that test? You're below average. You're going to flunk. You'll never amount to anything in life!"

"Why do you work so hard? You're so buried in bills, you can't get out of debt!"

"Your boss isn't happy with your last project. He's going to fire you. Why bother being so conscientious?"

"Why do you even attempt to train your children in the ways of God? You can't follow them yourself!"

"Why have you come out to line up for battle?"

Goliath was nothing but an ancient terrorist trying to intimidate people in order to get them to fight him on his own terms. He spoke the same language and utilized the same tactics satan uses against us continually: fear, manipulation, intimidation, derision, limitation, and rejection.

> *"Am I not a Philistine, and you the servants of Saul? Choose a man for yourselves, and let him come down to me. If he is able to fight with me and kill me, then we will be your servants. But if I prevail against him and kill him, then you shall be our servants and serve us." And the Philistine said, "I defy the armies of Israel this day; give me a man, that we may fight together." When Saul and Israel heard these words of the Philistine, they were dismayed and they were greatly afraid."*
> (1 Samuel 16:8-11)

Goliath's tactics worked. The entire army of Saul heard Goliath's challenge eighty times and did nothing about it! How could the Israelites have put up with this? Why would they not respond?

Confronting Goliath seemed to be an impossibility to every soldier, including King Saul. Everything about this giant--his outward appearance, his speech, his mannerisms, his stature, his demeanor—everything—stated, *"Goliath is too big for you to handle. You can't beat him, so stay away from him."*

And so for forty days, Goliath convinced the Israelites he was unbeatable; thus, he directed their focus toward the impossibility that loomed before them and *away* from God, His principles, and His promises.

The Bible makes it abundantly clear that God gave us the life we now live:

> *For You formed my inward parts;*
> *You covered me in my mother's womb. I will praise You, for I am fearfully and wonderfully made; Marvelous are Your works, And that my soul knows very well. My frame was not hidden from You when I was made in secret, and skillfully wrought in the lowest parts of the earth. Your eyes saw my substance, being yet unformed. And in Your book they all were written, the days fashioned for me, when as yet there were none of them.*
> (Psalm 139:13-16)

Along with life, our Heavenly Father gave us purpose. Long before our birth, God established a course for our lives. This truth is illustrated by the words God spoke to Jeremiah when the prophet was commissioned for service.

> *Before I formed you in the womb, I knew*
> *you; Before you were born I sanctified*
> *you; I ordained you a prophet to the na-*
> *tions.*
> (Jeremiah 1:5)

Moreover, our Heavenly Father designed us and equipped us *specifically* for the work He had for us to do on this earth, the work by which each of us would bring Him glory. Through the Holy Spirit, God has made available to us the gifts and tools by which we can fulfill our destiny.

We were created by God, we were created with purpose, and we have access to what is needed to carry out that purpose. Everything we are and everything we do hinges on our relationship with God. We are the most comfortable, confident, and effective when we are closest to God. We are most aware of what is available to us in Christ and what we can accomplish by His grace, when our relationship with our Heavenly Father is strong and secure.

In the first chapter of Ephesians, the Apostle Paul expresses his deep love and great respect for the believers in that church. He commends them for their faith in Christ and for the love they show one another. Then, Paul declares that as a result of having heard such great reports about the church, he prays for the Ephesian church continually.

> *"Therefore I also, after I heard of your*
> *faith in the Lord Jesus and your love for*

all the saints, do not cease to give thanks for you, making mention of you in my prayers:"
(Ephesians 1:15-16)

What did Paul ask God for continually regarding the church at Ephesus? What was Paul moved to pray for as he recognized the great character and good works of those believers?

He prayed that "the God of our Lord Jesus Christ, the Father of glory, may give to [them] the spirit of wisdom and revelation in the knowledge of Him, the eyes of [their] understanding being enlightened..."
(Ephesians 1:17)

For what purpose?

"That you may know what is the hope of His calling, what are the riches of the glory of His inheritance in the saints, and what is the exceeding greatness of His power toward us who believe, according to the working of His mighty power which He worked in Christ when He raised Him from the dead and seated Him at His right hand in the Heavenly places, far above all principality and power and might and dominion, and every name that is named, not only in

this age but also in that which is to come."
(Ephesians 1:18-21)

Paul continually gave thanks and prayed that God would reveal to the Ephesians more and more of His nature to them, whereby they would recognize the hope of Christ's calling, as well as the resources and the unlimited power that was available to them to fulfill that calling.

In other words, Paul's chief desire for his Ephesian brothers and sisters was for them to know God more intimately, and consequently, to understand how well-equipped they were in Him to carry out their life-mission.

The confidence and direction we need stems directly from our personal relationship with Christ. When our walk with God is solid, and we have a proper understanding of His nature, His love, and His blessings in our lives, we are perfectly poised to fulfill our destiny.

If we allow an impossibility to intimidate us, the impossibility will disrupt the flow of continual revelation of God; consequently, we will lose sight of the hope of our calling, our rich inheritance, and the divine power that is available to us. Any impossibility we run from will form a block between God and us, and it *will* impede our destiny.

In essence, Goliath stood in the Israelites' way, blocking their view of Jehovah—the God through whom all Goliaths can be toppled and victories can be won.

For forty days, Goliath put up a smoke screen, a veil that kept God's people from understanding and recognizing their identity, their purpose,

> Once their understanding of God and their identity in Him were tainted, Saul and his men could only evaluate their situation on earthly terms.

and their authority in Him. Once their understanding of God and their identity in Him were tainted, Saul and his men could only evaluate their situation on earthly terms. Instead of recognizing that they belonged to God, that this was His battle, and that He would enable them to win, Israel's army hid in their tents, saying, *"Goliath is bigger than we are. Goliath is stronger than we are. We can't beat him, so we won't fight him."*

The impossibilities we face in our lives, whatever they may be, will have the same negative effect on us, if we let them.

When we recognize that seemingly insurmountable obstacles have blocked our view of the Living God, we must begin to cry out to Him. We must contend in prayer for an encounter with God, an encounter which will generate within us an impossibility-defying perspective.

The question is never, *"How many does the opposing team or army have?"* Nor is the question, *"How strong are they, what weapons are in their arsenal, and what are the odds of beating them?"* The only question that really matters is, *"Who is going to rise up and confront the taunts and threats, overcome fear and intimidation, and trust God for the victory?"*

The question is not, *"Can you overcome the problem you're facing?"* The question is, *"Are you going to run toward it knowing that God is going to back you up as you do?"*

> The size of your challenge or problem can never limit God's grace and power. He is still bigger, and He is on your side.

If you are in God's army, you are going to have to fight some Goliaths. You *will* face the impossible, and when you do, remember that the size of your challenge or problem can never limit God's grace and power. He is still bigger, and He is on your side; His Word still says, *"All things are possible for those who believe."*

As I write this book, I see in my mind's eye a giant who has been standing in your way. For so long, you have not been able to look past the wall or smoke screen that has formed in front of you.

Your mind, will, and emotions have been consumed with fear and apprehension. The boldness and initiative God has placed within you have been held back by caution and concern. Every thought pattern leads you back to the giant standing in front of you, blocking your view and distorting your perception of your wonderful Heavenly Father.

My prayer for you is that as you continue to read this book, God's anointing will lift your burden and break the yoke of bondage. May He demolish the walls and lift the veils so you can see clearly the God who loves you, cares for you, and who is one hundred percent *for* you!

May all the blocks be lifted so you may know beyond a shadow of a doubt that nothing, *nothing* is impossible with Him!

CHAPTER 3

SMALL TASKS
AND
LARGE MOMENTS

B uilt within every child of God is the capacity to tackle and to conquer impossibilities.
It is like the homing instinct in geese. They
know when it is time to lift off en masse, form a
gigantic "V" in the sky, and head south. No one
teaches them. No one holds bird-migration semi-
nars, conferences, or retreats. Migrating birds operate by instinct.

The same applies for many other species with-in the animal kingdom, especially when it comes to food. Parents do not instruct their young how to seek nourishment; instead, they continually provide for them until they reach a certain age. Then the parents no longer share food with their young.

> Built within every child of God is the capacity to tackle and to conquer impossibilities.

Without ever having received any special training, the young mammals, birds, insects, etc., leave the "nest" and begin to provide for them-selves.

Seeking, finding, and obtaining food is built into many species; it is in their makeup. Likewise, every believer has within his or her spiritual makeup the potential and desire to conquer impossibility for the glory of God.

The fourteenth chapter of Matthew records a fascinating episode in the life of Jesus and the disciples. It occurred hours after the miraculous feeding of five thousand men.

> *And when He had sent the multitudes away, He went up on the mountain by Himself to pray. Now when evening came, He was alone there. But the boat was now in the middle of the sea,[a] tossed by the waves, for the wind was contrary. Now in the fourth watch of the night Jesus went to them, walking on the sea. And when the disciples saw Him walking on the sea, they were troubled, saying, "It is a ghost!" And they cried out for fear. But immediately Jesus spoke to them, saying, "Be of good cheer! It is I; do not be afraid." And Peter answered Him and said, "Lord, if it is You, command me to come to You on the water."*
> (Matthew 14:23-28)

I find Peter's request strange.

Peter and the rest of the disciples in the boat thought they saw a ghost walking on the waters of the large lake. The "ghost" spoke to them, saying *"Cheer up (Jesus' characteristic greeting.) It's just Me; don't be afraid."*

Obviously, Peter was not convinced. He was still afraid, so he asked, *"If it is you, command me to come to you on the water."*

If I thought there was a ghost on the lake posing as the Lord, and I was trying to validate the being's true identity, I can't see myself wanting to leave my companions, step out of a boat, and walk on water towards whatever was out there. Peter *did!*

Peter could only find peace and security in being where Jesus was, doing what Jesus was doing.

The reason for Peter's bold request and the "leap of faith" that followed was that Peter could only find peace and security in being where Jesus was, doing what Jesus was doing. The only way for Peter's fear and apprehension to be eradicated was to venture out to Jesus, even if it meant risking everything by trying to walk on water.

Peter had within him a natural inclination towards the miraculous, the supernatural, the impossible. Without any time to think this through, out of the abundance of what was within him, Peter put in his request and took his first step to-wards the impossible.

Every Spirit-filled believer in Jesus has the same yearning and the same potential for the mi-raculous. The Holy Spirit living inside us prompts us to take bold steps towards the impossible. Any-thing less is simply unacceptable to us. It is *"hope deferred"* and ultimately it *"makes the heart sick."*

We have every reason to be bold in the face of im-possibility, especially when we know and live by the Word of the Lord:

> *"Who shall separate us from the love of Christ? Shall trouble or hardship or per-secution or famine or nakedness or dan-ger or sword?"*
> (Romans 8:35)

Much of what constitutes famines, nakedness, dangers, swords, and perils qualifies as impossi-bility. Therefore, the question, *"Who can separate us from the love of Christ?"* can be rephrased as, *"Are there any impossibilities that the love of Christ, work-ing in and through us, cannot overcome?"*

> *"No, in all these things we are more than conquerors through Him who loved us."*
> (Romans 8:37)

As we face all these *impossibilities*, we are more than conquerors through Him who loved us. This verse does not say Christ is more than a conqueror (though He is.) It emphasizes that *"We* are more than conquerors through *Him* who loved us." *We* are the conquerors!

David was born to kill giants, defeat armies, and conquer territory for His God, yet David had no idea about any of his intrinsic capacity for conquest. That which had been deposited by God in David did not manifest itself until the young shepherd came face to face with the impossibility named Goliath.

We don't know exactly how the battle of David and Goliath ensued, but here's a likely scenario:

Shortly after David arrived at the Israelites' camp, he was visiting with his brothers when suddenly he heard Goliath's propaganda speech. David witnessed firsthand the avoid-confrontation-at-all-cost stance of the Israelite army. Without even thinking about it (just like Peter in the boat), David made a decision to fight Goliath.

It is important to note that when David left his father's house to head towards the Valley of Elam, he did not think about encountering, challenging, facing, fighting, killing, and decapitating a Philistine giant. It was never on his agenda. What *was* on David's agenda was the rather insignificant task of delivering a care package to his brothers and bringing back a report to his father!

Then Jesse said to his son David, "Take now for your brothers an ephah of this dried grain and these ten loaves, and run to your brothers at the camp. And carry these ten cheeses to the captain of their thousand, and see how your brothers fare, and bring back news of them."
(1 Samuel 17:17)

On the day that David fought Goliath, he had two assignments. His first task was from David's earthly father; the second was from his Heavenly Father.

God's assignment for David was to conquer the impossible by confronting and ultimately destroying the man who had been taunting the armies of Israel for forty days. God had ordained for David to defeat Goliath and consequently to rout the Philistines. God had destined David to be the catalyst for Israel's victory.

Yet David did not know anything about his God-given assignment until he actually arrived at the battlefield. What led David to the battlefield was the assignment from his father, Jesse.

There was nothing exciting or glorious about delivering cheese and grain and returning with a report. The task required no supernatural help and no special anointing or skill. It only required a certain character quality—one that from the day

Adam was created to this day has made all the difference in every God-ordained pursuit: obedience.

David came face to face with the *im*possible while being faithful and obedient to do that which was possible. His faithfulness in the small task brought David into a larger moment, which then launched him into his destiny.

The same principle spans the ages from David's time to ours, and it applies to our lives today. While being obedient and faithful to fulfill our daily or weekly obligations, we encounter circumstances by which God reveals more of His will and plan for our lives.

The "giant" before us will either stall our spiritual progress if we avoid it, or thrust us deeper into our destiny if we confront it.

While being obedient to perform routine, mundane, or even undesirable tasks, we suddenly find ourselves face to face with impossibility. The "giant" before us will either stall our spiritual progress if we avoid it, or thrust us deeper into our destiny if we confront it. Either way, being faithful and obedient gets us to the place where we have the opportunity for victory and ultimately increase in favor and influence within God's Kingdom.

Jesus told the disciples before He ascended into heaven, *"Go stay in Jerusalem and wait for the promise of the Father."* (Acts 1:4) In obedience, they went into an upper room, and for ten days, they did what Jesus told them to do. They waited.

Waiting is not a task that requires supernatural ability or input from the Heavenly realm; however, it does require inner spiritual strength, in the form of obedience, patience, temperance, and self-control.

For ten days, the disciples prayed and they waited in an upper room. Then in Acts, Chapter 2, at the beginning of that chapter, we read this verse. "And suddenly there came a sound from heaven, as of a rushing mighty wind..." While they were doing the thing they *could* do, heaven invaded and they started to experience and operate in what they could *not* do. In fact, their experience was greater than they could ever imagine. This sudden breakthrough came after these believers proved themselves obedient and faithful in their assignment.

Gideon is another example of a man in the Bible who is thrust into his destiny while just doing his job. When we meet Gideon, he is threshing wheat. Suddenly, an angel comes and stands right beside him saying, *"Gideon, you are a mighty man of valor."* (Judges 6:12)

What happened? Suddenly, Gideon was introduced to an impossibility (leading an Israelite army against the vast Midianite army) that would launch him into his destiny.

Similarly, Moses was tending sheep on the backside of a desert for his father-in-law, Jethro, when he suddenly noticed a bush that was burning, yet not being consumed. He heard a voice coming out of the bush.

> *"Take the sandals off of your feet, the ground you're standing on is Holy ground." (Exodus 3:5)*

We never find Moses tending sheep again. From the moment when the Voice spoke, Moses was thrust into his destiny to *"deliver [God's] people from slavery in Egypt."(Exodus 3:10)*

The staff turning to a snake, the leprous hand being restored, the ten plagues, the release of Egypt's wealth, the parting of the Red Sea, the annihilation of the Egyptian army, the provision of food and water in the wilderness, the pillar of cloud and the pillar of fire to guide the people...Moses encountered and overcame one impossibility after another by the grace and power of the Living God. How did it all start? A shepherd in the desert, tending sheep, being faithful in doing his job, was ushered into the realm of impossibility.

So it was with David. What propelled David into God's plan for his life – not only to lead troops to battle, but also to lead a nation of God's people for fifty years – was the killing of Goliath. The mundane act that brought David to the place where he would encounter and ultimately destroy Goliath was taking cheese and grain to his brothers.

Don't despise the day of small beginnings, friend! Don't ever think that what you are doing is not significant. God will set your destiny in motion while you are being faithful to accomplish what He assigns to you day after day.

Look at the challenges of your life. I'm not talking about the things you can do by your ability, your own effort, your own determination. I'm talking about the impossible stuff!

You may have perceived your challenges to fulfilling your dreams as roadblocks or dead ends. If so, stop thinking that way right now. Look at challenges as on-ramps to the highway of your destiny.

The small task brought David to a large moment. David seized the moment. It is important to recognize the opportunities available in every situation and to take advantage of them. The key to being able to recognize such opportunities is having the right perspective—a godly perspective. David did!

> *And all the men of Israel, when they saw*
> *the man, fled from him and were dread-*
> *fully afraid. So the men of Israel said,*
> *"Have you seen this man who has come*
> *up? Surely he has come up to defy Israel;*
> *and it shall be that the man who kills him*
> *the king will enrich with great riches,*
> *will give him his daughter, and give his*
> *father's house exemption from taxes in*
> *Israel."*
> (1 Samuel 17:24)

No taxes! *There's* a great incentive to take on any giant!

> *Then David spoke to the men who stood*
> *by him, saying, "What shall be done for*
> *the man who kills this Philistine and*
> *takes away the reproach from Israel?*
> (verse 26)

While the minds of Israel's fighters were focused on the impossibility of toppling the Philistine warrior, David's mind was already beyond the battle and even the victory; his mind was on the reward!

There was never a question in David's mind regarding the outcome of the duel. In his eyes, Goliath was just another *"uncircumcised Philistine,"* who dared *"defy the armies of the living God."* Goliath would undoubtedly lose; hence David's question, *"What's the prize for killing him?"*

Why did David see it like that? Why was David different than the rest of the army of Israel including the king, Saul?

It was because David knew God more intimately than anybody else there! While shepherding his sheep on the hills of Bethlehem, David developed a vibrant relationship with Jehovah. He prayed the prayers and sang the songs we find in the book of Psalms. He learned to depend on God for the strength and the anointing to defend sheep against predators.

Goliath was the personification of impossibility; David was the personification of a worshipper!

Long before Jesus ever spoke to the woman by the well and said, *"You shall worship the Lord in spirit and in truth,"* (John 4:24) David was modeling that very lifestyle of worship.

Goliath was the personification of impossibility; David was the personification of a worshipper! A worshipper will always topple impossibility, because through worship, he strengthens his relationship with the God who trumps all impossibility, the God with whom all things are possible!

David knew the Living God; therefore, he understood the principle that if God was for him, no one could stand against him. That made all the difference.

When we know God, when we spend time with Him, when we invoke Him in all the affairs of our lives, our small tasks will lead to large moments when we will face the impossible. In those moments, I urge you to run toward the impossibility, knowing that God is with you. If you know Him, if you love Him, if you honor Him, the Lord your God is with you. *No one* can prevail against you!

CHAPTER 4

PRESSING THROUGH

Finding the courage to take on seemingly impossible challenges is a positive step forward, but it is not the whole battle. Most times, another formidable foe must be toppled before we can even tackle the impossible.

As imposing and as intimidating as Goliath may have appeared, and as formidable an enemy as he may have been, Goliath was not David's worst opponent that day at the Valley of Elam.

The moment David saw Goliath and heard his boastful words, he determined in his heart to confront him. David's decision was instinctive and instantaneous. Yet, before David would put five smooth stones in his pouch, take his sling, and start running toward the impossible, he had to face off with the deadly giants of fear, unbelief, criticism, and negativity. Moreover, David had to press through the opposition stemming from his own countrymen, especially his own brothers.

> Now Eliab, his oldest brother, heard when he spoke to the men; and Eliab's anger was aroused against David, and he said, "Why did you come down here? And with whom have you left those few sheep in the wilderness? I know your

*pride and the insolence of your heart, for
you have come down to see the battle."*
(1 Samuel 17:28)

David's resolve to fight Goliath invoked a mental offense in David's oldest brother, Eliab. The thought of David confronting the Philistine warrior ran contrary to Eliab's perception of his little brother. Therefore, Eliab voiced his opposition to David's plan by trying to place limitations over him.

"David, you are here as the delivery boy for grain and cheese. You are a shepherd, not a fighter. You have no business being on a battlefield, much less taking on Goliath. Go back to your sheep, David, and leave the fighting to the professionals!"

Moreover, Eliab used manipulation to distract David's mind from the battle back to the hills of Bethlehem — where, according to Eliab, David truly *belonged*.

Eliab knew that David had a heart for his sheep. Perhaps he had even heard the stories of David having fought lions and bears to save the sheep from being devoured. Therefore, Eliab attempted to plant a seed of concern in David's mind for his flock back home.

"With whom did you leave your sheep?"

"Your sheep are most likely not as well attended as they would be when you are with them. They may even

be in danger, David. You had better stop talking this nonsense about confronting Goliath, and get back to your sheep!"

Finally, David's brother even took a shot at David's character saying, *"I know the pride of your heart, the insolence of your heart. You came out here just to watch a fight!"* (1 Samuel 17:28)

Why did Eliab use intimidation, humiliation, manipulation, and accusation to limit David and keep him from attempting the impossible? Primarily, it was because those were the forces dominating Eliab. Jesus said, *"Out of the abundance of the heart, the mouth speaks."* (Matthew 12:34) What is within comes out, especially in crisis.

Men and women who operate under fear and limitation will project that same fear and limitation over anyone who demonstrates a desire to take on the impossible, and thus get free from the clutches of destiny-hindering forces.

Misery loves company. Fear-driven folks cannot deal with the thought of seeing their impossibility-defying brothers and sisters wrench themselves free from what has held *them* back.

David's resolve to fight Goliath was met with opposition by the very people who were unwilling to fight the Philistine themselves, and, particularly, who were unwilling to accept the prospect of *David* doing it. Everyone wanted Goliath killed; they just didn't want the young and (seemingly) tenderhearted shepherd to show them up.

> When you decide to dream big and attempt the impossible, expect opposition, especially from those who have stopped dreaming long ago.

Everybody wants challenges overcome and victories won, but many people are not comfortable watching *you* do it, especially if they have already missed their own opportunity to do so.

When you decide to dream big and attempt the impossible, expect opposition, especially from those who have stopped dreaming long ago. They will criticize from the sidelines, giving you all the reasons why you should not think and operate that way. They will tell you how ministering to people at church or on the job, praying for the sick, leading folks to Christ, and making an impact in your generation is not for you.

"You're just a shepherd, a delivery boy. Those jobs are for the apostles, the prophets, the pastors, the evan-

gelists, and the teachers; those who are trained to be world-changers."

And yet, Ephesians, 11:14-16 says:

> *It was he who gave some to be apostles, some to be prophets, some to be evangelists, and some to be pastors and teachers, to prepare God's people for works of service, so that the body of Christ may be built up until we all reach unity in the faith and in the knowledge of the Son of God and become mature, attaining to the whole measure of the fullness of Christ. Then we will no longer be infants, tossed back and forth by the waves, and blown here and there by every wind of teaching and by the cunning and craftiness of men in their deceitful scheming. Instead, speaking the truth in love, we will in all things grow up into him who is the Head, that is, Christ. From him the whole body, joined and held together by every supporting ligament, grows and builds itself up in love, as each part does its work.*

As a pastor, I have never, ever perceived people in my congregation as second-class citizens when it comes to the anointing, divine purpose, and being used of the Holy Spirit for the glory of God. Yes, I am called to lead, but we are all fighting side by side on the front lines. My job is not to condescend others or build pedestals for me to stand on; it is to facilitate an atmosphere where people will seek the face of God, first and foremost, and then out of that place of intimacy with Christ become equipped to fight on the front lines alongside me.

I love David's response to Eliab:

And David said, "What have I done now? *Is there* not a cause?" I Samuel 17:29

"I thought we had something worth fighting for here, a mission, a mandate from heaven. I thought we were God's people, 'the head and not the tail.' Is there not a cause?!"

David, obviously not hearing a response from Eliab, appealed to the other soldiers standing by:

Fear, negativity, criticism, and unbelief are contagious, just like faith is!

Then he turned from him toward another and said the same thing; and these people answered him as the first ones did. (1 Samuel 17:30)

"...these people answered him as the first ones did!"

I'm not surprised!

Fear, negativity, criticism, and unbelief are contagious, just like faith is!

If one person has faith and starts to preach faith, teach faith, talk faith, live faith, and breathe faith, it will spread. Then fear is lifted, faith takes over, and anything can happen!

The same dynamic is in place when attitudes of fear and unbelief enter. They seep into the crowd, and people start doubting, questioning, wondering, *"Hmm, Goliath is bigger...David, you know, he is not a trained fighter, he hasn't had a lot of Philistine-slaying experience!"*

In the thirteenth chapter of Numbers we find another example of the conflict between faith and negativity. The Lord was instructing Moses to explore the land of Canaan, the land He was giving His people. Twelve spies were sent, one leader from each ancestral tribe of Israel.

Two of the twelve men came back with the following perspective, *"The land is good. Look at the grapes! Look at the pomegranates, look at all the good stuff from the land. God told us we could take it! Let's go get it!"*

The other ten spies had the opposite opinion:

> *But the men who had gone up with him said, "We can't attack those people; they are stronger than we are." And they spread among the Israelites a bad report about the land they had explored. They said, "The land we explored devours those living in it. All the people we saw*

there are of great size. We saw the Ne-
philim there (the descendants of Anak
come from the Nephilim). We seemed like
grasshoppers in our own eyes, and we
looked the same to them."
(Numbers 13:31-33)

The masses believed the ten! Every one of them died in the Promised Land, except the two *"Joshua, the son of Nun, and Caleb, the son of Jephunneh..."*

Why did the millions die and miss out on the Promise? Because of their fear and unbelief!

Fear and unbelief are contagious. Criticism, complaining, and backbiting are contagious. And that is why when I sense or encounter any such sentiments I do everything possible to avoid the individuals who spawn them.

I am committed to doing everything possible to maintain love in my heart for all people, regardless of their behavior or mindset. I will always do my best to love those who are negative, accusatory, critical, skeptical, and judgmental; however, they will never be my friends.

Running to impossibilities is contingent in large measure on establishing and maintaining a support system of friends, advisors, and mentors who are encouragers, faith builders, dream enhancers, and positive thinkers.

God has blessed me with many wonderful friends. I love each of them for many different reasons, and I thank the Lord for everyone. I am especially grateful for the inspiration I receive from my friends in the area of faith and courage. I have one very good friend, whom I consider the most fearless adventurer when it comes to launching into uncharted waters. This man is the ultimate pioneer in 'my book', completely fearless in the face of the unknown.

When he believes God is leading him to pursue a particular venture—ministry and/or business—he wholeheartedly embraces it, plans for it, and engages all his energy and resources to bring it to fruition. Though my friend faces many challenges along the way, fear of failure is never one of them.

From time to time, I call my friend and arrange to spend time with him. During our times together, I encourage him to talk about his projects and pursuits. Just listening to him stretches me beyond my comfort zone. Fear and limitation depart from me when I am in the presence of this man. I leave our meetings enriched and changed for the glory of God.

Here is my advice: always love and respect all people, especially if you are in a position of leadership, but only befriend those who will push you forward in the pursuit of your God-given destiny.

David had no one in his corner at the Valley of Elam. He was surrounded by individuals who employed defamation of character, demeaning words, intimidation, fear tactics, and humiliation to try to stop David from doing something great for God's Kingdom.

Yet, David was undaunted. His mind was made up to fight Goliath, and no naysayer would stop him.

After rejecting the negative advice from the crowd, the ambitious shepherd was summoned to King Saul's tent. Saul's approach was different from Eliab's; the king tried to reason with David:

> And Saul said to David, "You are not able to go against this Philistine to fight with him; for you are a youth, and he a man of war from his youth."
> (1 Samuel 17:33)

In essence, "David, the numbers don't add up. He's been fighting since he was a kid. You are a kid! You cannot fight him."

David's response to the king is one of the most inspiring portions in the Bible:

> But David said to Saul, "Your servant used to keep his father's sheep, and when a lion or a bear came and took a lamb out of the flock, I went out after it and struck it, and delivered the lamb from its

mouth; and when it arose against me, I caught it by its beard, and struck and killed it. Your servant has killed both lion and bear; and this uncircumcised Philistine will be like one of them, seeing he has defied the armies of the living God." Moreover, David said, "The LORD, who delivered me from the paw of the lion and from the paw of the bear, He will deliver me from the hand of this Philistine." (1 Samuel 17:34-37)

David's resolve prevailed. Saul finally conceded. *"Go and God be with you,"* the king said.

Both men talked of the same God—Jehovah, the God of the Bible. Yet, their perception of God was very different. Saul's farewell, *"...and God be with you,"* reflects Saul's mindset—*"May God be with you in that moment when you face Goliath."* David's perspective was that God was with him *continually*; therefore, he was assured of victory against Goliath.

The God who had been with David when he confronted lions and bears, was with him, regardless of the challenge, the obstacle, or the impossibility before him. David had absorbed one of the most important principles of God's Kingdom, "God is always for and with those who love Him and honor Him through their lives." The difference between Saul's mindset and David's mindset was the difference between failure and success in the confrontation with the Philistines at the Valley of Elam!

I pray God will enlighten the eyes of your understanding to grab hold of this truth and never let go of it: God is *for* you, He is *with* you, He has already set you up to succeed, and through Jesus Christ, He assures you of the victory. All you have left to do is run to the battle.

God has been, is now, and always will be *with* you!

CHAPTER 5

FINAL HURDLE

David pressed through the criticism of his brothers and the skepticism of King Saul, and he remained unwavering in his determination to fight Goliath. Yet, even after the king agreed to let David move forward with his plans, there was one more obstacle to overcome. The hurdle came in the form of a kind offer from the king for David to wear the king's armor and use his sword against the Philistine warrior.

> *So Saul clothed David with his armor, and he put a bronze helmet on his head; he also clothed him with a coat of mail. David fastened his sword to his armor and tried to walk, for he had not tested them.* (1 Samuel 17:38-39)

I so appreciate David's response to the armor-loaner offer:

> *"I cannot walk with these, for I have not tested them." So David took them off.*
> (1 Samuel 17:38)

In essence David was saying, *"It doesn't fit me ...I can't be wearing this. ...this is not me."*

I once heard it said, *"You can't tune one piano to another piano."* It is impossible to have two pianos side by side and tune them to produce the exact same sound. Each piano has its own distinct sound.

Likewise, no two individuals respond to and confront impossibilities in the same exact way.

When I first started preaching, I used my last dollars many times to buy the weekly sermon tapes of a well-known, highly respected, and very successful preacher. I listened to at least two tapes every week. Being young, green, and very impressionable, I quickly fell into the trap of developing a style that was not mine.

I loved what I was hearing, and I loved the response this pastor was getting, especially during his altar calls. He would start on one side of the floor, move to the other side, and finally to the balcony, acknowledging the hands being raised for Christ. Sometimes there were dozens of people saved in one service.

I was so eager to see such results and so convinced that his impeccable oratory skills influenced his success that I started to "borrow" some of the phrases, mannerisms, and idioms of this minister. Before long, I was taking entire sections of his sermons, reworking them a bit, and preaching them as though they stemmed from personal revelation and encounter with God.

The people I ministered to may not have perceived or minded the radical changes my preaching style and content were undergoing, but there was one individual who was neither amused nor persuaded.

My wife has always been my best encourager and greatest cheerleader. On the other hand, she has never hesitated to lovingly speak a word of constructive criticism. Better yet, she has always had a special way of communicating (from the pew) her discomfort with my "performance." Whenever I operated in a mode that was foreign to my own personality and gifting, Danielle's body language and expression let me know she was onto me. She did not have to say anything; I just knew from her demeanor that I was off base.

One Wednesday morning, my wife happened to drive my car and she came upon a preaching tape that I had left in the tape player. She pressed the play button, listened for a while, and quickly became aware of the source of much of my preaching material. That same night, an unexpected emergency rendered my pastor unable to attend the service. On the spur of a moment, I ended up in the pulpit. I did not have time to prepare thoroughly, plus I had the mindset that it was "just" a Wednesday night service so I could "talk instead of preach." Thus, I would save all the "good stuff" I had received from the preaching tapes for a "bigger service," perhaps a Sunday morning or a Sunday evening assignment (Mercy Lord!).

As it turned out that evening, I spoke out of my heart about what the Lord had shown me in His Word that very same day. It was by no means polished or rehearsed. (During that time in my life, I would normally take time to rehearse my messages word for word before preaching.) I felt extremely uncomfortable the entire time I was speaking.

When we got home that evening, Danielle lifted my bowed head, kissed me on the lips, and said, *"That's the best I ever heard you preach. There is absolutely no need for you to try so hard to be like somebody else. God speaks to you and through you just the same."*

It also took years to fully understand how accurate my wife was with that statement. Yet, I received her reproof, and it changed me.

At times, we may be able to acquire certain traits from people. We may even emulate a few qualities or characteristics we like; however, we must never compromise or downgrade our own divinely-apportioned gifts and abilities. We should learn from others, and can even try various methods that have worked for others, but first and foremost, we should rely on what our Heavenly Father deposited in us.

What God had established in David's heart and life was far more potent than any armor or weapon he could borrow from Saul. David declined the king's offer, and thereby overcame the last hurdle propped up between himself and the impossible—Goliath.

When you start running toward the impossible, you will meet opposition and criticism. You may even encounter the same hurdle David faced: the temptation to emulate others at the expense of your own initiative, drive, and anointing.

... you must not let anyone infringe upon your destiny. You cannot change your course just because somebody doesn't believe in you.

How will you overcome these challenges? What are you going to do when the opinions of Eliabs and King Sauls stand between you and the impossibilities you want to conquer?

First and foremost, you must not let anyone infringe upon your destiny. You cannot change your course just because somebody doesn't believe in you. Your Heavenly Father who believes in you more than all of the others combined, resoundingly and emphatically says, *"Through Christ, you can do anything!"*

Secondly, you have to consider the source of the criticism. Those who are not giant-fighters or giant-killers and those who would rather hide in a trench for forty days than confront Goliaths, have no credibility to tell those of us who want to fight giants that we can't do it!

Instead of being a good example of an older brother to David and modeling courage, boldness, and bravery in the face of impossibility, Eliab became the chief spokesperson against David's plans. However, Eliab had no right to give an opinion; his cowardice during the forty days of Goliath's taunts and threats had stripped him of any authority or influence in the matter.

It is OK if the fearful and the critics do not want to fight the giant. It is OK if they want to run away and hide from impossibilities. It is OK for them to remain out of sight until the victory is won and then come out for the celebration—I can live with all that. But, it is not OK for these individuals to insist that those who are called to fight giants not even try!

So what should we do in the face of such unqualified critics? We must love, respect, and honor our brothers and sisters, but we must also obey the promptings and directives of God within our hearts and lives. If the critics and the skeptics are not giant-killers, they have no grounds for telling us we cannot run to impossibilities.

Thirdly, and most importantly, we must not judge those who oppose us. Throughout this encounter with his brothers and the rest of the army, David never defended himself. They called him proud, insolent of heart, and they demeaned him saying, *"You will never be anything but a shepherd."* Yet, David did not react. He did not snap back at them. He did not retaliate. David's only response was, *"I thought we had a cause here. I thought we were fighting for something."*

Moreover, David did not judge his king. He could have contended, *"You are the King of Israel; you ought to know better than that! You're the King of Israel; you haven't done anything for forty days. How can you tell me I can't fight Goliath?"* David honored the authority over him, and he honored his brothers. He did not judge anyone.

The Church should learn from David's attitude in this encounter. A move of God will end prematurely when people who grow spiritually by leaps and bounds, scrutinize or criticize those who may not be growing at the same rate.

When the Holy Spirit began to move mightily upon our congregation at Valley Shore in Old Saybrook, CT, I issued (and frequently reiterated) the following statement:

"We are standing before a river of God's blessing. The Lord assures us this is good water, and His desire for us is to be refreshed, renewed, and invigorated by a mighty outpouring of His Spirit. Yet, I want you to know that as far as I am concerned, you are free to go in as far as you want to go in.

"Some of you may be hesitant or apprehensive. You may wish to stand along the banks of the river and watch. Some of you may want to enter only up to your toes. Others may go in up to the ankles or the knees. Some of you will go waist-deep, maybe even up to the shoulders. As for my wife, my children, and me, we are diving in head first, and we encourage you to join us; however, if you choose not to, we will still love you with all our hearts and we will continue to serve, honor, and care for you as our brothers and sisters in Christ."

> Judging those who may appear unspiritual or less spiritual will kill a revival.

Judging those who may appear unspiritual or less spiritual will kill a revival. Loving everyone the same, regardless of their views or disposition towards the things of God, will keep the revival growing. Eventually, the fire will spread far enough to warm and ignite even some of the coldest hearts. Never, ever judge anyone, especially your critics.

No one modeled this principle better than our Lord, Jesus:

> *Nevertheless, even among the rulers many believed in Him, but because of the Pharisees they did not confess Him, lest*

they should be put out of the synagogue;
for they loved the praise of men more
than the praise of God.
Then Jesus cried out and said, "He who
believes in Me, believes not in Me but in
Him who sent Me. And he who sees Me
sees Him who sent Me. I have come as a
light into the world, that whoever be-
lieves in Me should not abide in dark-
ness. And if anyone hears My words and
does not believe, I do not judge him; for I
did not come to judge the world but to
save the world."
(John 12:42-47)

Jesus is saying this! He is saying that He left heaven, came to this earth as a baby, grew up as a man, and lived a blameless, sinless life. *He* is telling us, *"I did not come to judge you!"*

If Jesus is not willing to judge people, then who are we to do so? Not everyone can handle Goliath, and they may even act dishonorably by trying to stop us from fighting. Yet, if they believe that Jesus died, rose again, and saves sinners, they are our brothers and sisters in Christ. Even if they flow in a different stream than the one we may be flowing in, even if they do not believe that miracles are for today or that tongues are of God, they are still our brothers and sisters in Christ. Honoring, respecting, and loving our opposition is one of the key ingredients for a lasting revival.

David successfully mastered the three aspects of the challenges mentioned in the previous paragraphs. In the face of all the opposition from all the individuals surrounding him, David made preparation for the fight. The following verse is pivotal in this encounter:

> *Then, with his staff in his hand, he chose for himself five smooth stones from the brook, put them in a shepherd's bag – a pouch that he had, and with his sling in his hand he drew near to the Philistine.*
> (1 Samuel 17:40)

I believe in that moment when David put the stones in his pouch, all of heaven knew David would win regardless which stone he picked or where he flung it. He had passed the test. He had pressed through all the barriers people had placed in front of him, and he set his face like a flint on the confrontation with Goliath.

I can never prove this, so I ask the reader to be gracious—it is just my opinion. That stone would have hit Goliath no matter where David threw it. David hit the mark and won the day, because God determined, "David, *you're going to win no matter what you do."* Armed with a slingshot and five stones, and backed by all the resources of heaven, David was ready for the fight.

Let us read once again the central verse for this book:

> So it was, when the Philistine arose and came and drew near to meet David that David hurried and ran toward the army to meet the Philistine.
> (1 Samuel 17:48)

Every step he took towards Goliath brought David closer to his destiny.

Why did David run towards the Philistine? Primarily, David ran because every step he took towards Goliath brought David closer to his destiny.

Moreover, while David ran *towards* the Philistine, he was also running *from* his critics — those who thought he should not even be there. David was running towards the call of God and away from those who wanted to stop him from pursuing it. No wonder he ran — I would have run too!

I'd rather sprint toward a giant that could crush me with one finger, believing God to help me, than to listen to the critics and skeptics who want to deter me from trying.

When you decide to do something impossible for God, be prepared for those who will come to tell you why it can't be done, why it can't be done just then, why it can't be done the way you are planning to do it, and especially why *you* can't do it.

Anytime you start to dream, expect the dream killers to show up next. Every time you tell your brothers and sisters the great dreams God gave you, be prepared to be mocked, criticized, maybe even thrown into a pit like Joseph.

Dream Killers—they're out there! That's why you have to be careful with whom you share your dreams. Talk to the dream builders! Talk to the dream makers! Don't talk to dream killers until it is absolutely necessary to do so. Then contend for what your God-given destiny demands of you, and run to the battle with boldness.

What God told you to do, what's in your heart to do, what you're dreaming about, can be threatened, jolted, and shaken, but it can never be eradicated. If God gave it to you, your dream can never be killed. The only way it will die is if you bury it by quitting.

Don't quit! If you don't quit, in time the Lord our God will give you the victory.

CHAPTER 6

THE MOTIVE

L et us quickly review what has already taken place in our narrative of the events on the battlefield at the Valley of Elam.

Goliath challenged the Israelites to fight him. For forty days, Saul and his army heard Goliath's insults and taunts, but did nothing. Driven by fear, they chose to remain in their tents and listen to Goliath's propaganda. In their minds, the Philistine giant was unbeatable. Goliath was the personification of the impossible for Saul and his men.

David arrived at the Israelite camp to deliver food to his brothers and their officers. While visiting with the men, David heard Goliath's challenge and immediately determined in his heart to fight Goliath.

A wave of opposition to David's plans followed. His brothers and all their comrades tried to convince David that he was incapable of handling such a confrontation. King Saul himself was involved, expressing his own concerns about the apparent mismatch between David and Goliath.

David finally convinced Saul to allow him to fight. He made preparations, gathering five smooth stones for his sling, and then he ran towards his enemy—he ran towards the impossible.

It is important to note that the events surrounding the battle between David and Goliath happened quickly. They all took place within a few hours on one day, though it may seem that more time is involved because we are looking at the incident over the course of several chapters, taking the time to analyze the dynamics and break down the story in order to receive insight from the various aspects of the encounter.

Analysis aside, here's what basically happened: David walked onto the battlefield, saw and heard Goliath, decided to fight him, and talked it over with his people for a while. Within hours David ran to the battle. By the time the sun had set that day, Goliath was dead, the Philistines had been routed, and the matter was closed.

I draw attention to the actual sequence of events to spotlight an important Kingdom principle. When we come face to face with the impossible in our lives, we don't always have time to weigh the odds, consider all the possibilities, and make a well-thought out decision. We often don't have time to evaluate the matter against the context of our life and calling, and thus decide whether or not we should move forward. In fact, most times, we don't even have time to "pray about it."

The capacity to run *to* the impossibilities we face rather than run *from* them is either in us or it is not. We will either be repelled by or attracted to the impossible.

David did not take time to contemplate how "unthinkable" it was for him to fight and destroy such a formidable foe as Goliath. The experiences of his life had conditioned David to run into such challenges head-on.

> David developed a keen understanding of God's ways, he trusted in God's support, and therefore he was bold, very bold!

David was exposed to what was happening and immediately said, *"I'm going for it!"* David's boldness and courage in that moment, as well as his unwavering decision to fight Goliath in spite of all the opposition he faced, stemmed from the well-established, vibrant personal relationship David had with God.

Through his lifestyle of passionate worship, wholehearted devotion, and consistent obedience, David cultivated a special friendship with the Living God. David developed a keen understanding of God's ways, he trusted in God's support, and therefore he was bold, very bold! Not once in the course of David's lifetime do we read that David hesitated in the face of impossibilities.

Relationship with God is everything. When we have confidence in God due to a solid walk with Him, we never need much time to think about whether or not we should take on giants.

The four gospels are replete with examples of Jesus confronting impossibilities. With the exception of the raising of Lazarus (where the Lord offered a prayer that everyone could hear), none of the Lord's miracles were preceded by lengthy, passionate prayers.

A remarkable illustration of his pattern of operation is found in Mark 9. Upon his return from the mountain where He was transfigured in front of Peter, James, and John, Jesus met a man who was desperate for His assistance:

> *"Teacher, I brought You my son, who has a mute spirit. And wherever it seizes him, it throws him down; he foams at the mouth, gnashes his teeth, and becomes rigid. So I spoke to Your disciples, that they should cast it out, but they could not."*
> (Mark 9:17-18)

Jesus commenced work on the problem immediately:

> *So He asked his father, "How long has this been happening to him?"*
> *And he said, "From childhood. And often he has thrown him both into the fire and*

*into the water to destroy him. But if You
can do anything, have compassion on us
and help us."*

*Jesus said to him, "If you can believe,[a]
all things are possible to him who believes." Immediately the father of the
child cried out and said with tears,
"Lord, I believe; help my unbelief!"*

*When Jesus saw that the people came
running together, He rebuked the un-
clean spirit, saying to it, "Deaf and
dumb spirit, I command you, come out of
him and enter him no more!" Then the
spirit cried out, convulsed him greatly,
and came out of him. And he became as
one dead, so that many said, "He is
dead." But Jesus took him by the hand
and lifted him up, and he arose.*
(Mark 9:20-27)

After the incident was behind them, the disciples approached Jesus with a question:

*"Why could we not cast it out?"
So He said to them, "This kind can come
out by nothing but prayer and fasting."*
(Mark 9:29)

The prayer and fasting that prepared Jesus'
heart for this and every other impossibility He
faced, took place long before Jesus encountered the
individuals and their problems.

In Luke 5 we get some insight into Jesus' prayer life:

> *However, the report went around con-*
> *cerning Him all the more; and great*
> *multitudes came together to hear, and to*
> *be healed by Him of their infirmities. So*
> *He Himself often withdrew into the wil-*
> *derness and prayed.*
> (Luke 5:15-16)

The key word is the word "so" in verse 16. The NIV uses the word "but" instead. In the context of verse 15, the word "so" (or "but") is transitional in nature. Jesus' popularity and influence increased dramatically, and quickly; therefore (*so*), He often pulled away from the crowds to be alone with the Father in prayer.

Jesus had to get away from the multitudes that were crowding Him in order to pray. He needed to recharge and be refreshed by the Father; however, Jesus also had to get away and pray in order to prepare for the next wave of hungry, desperate seekers — the folks He would encounter once he returned to the "battlefield."

By the time Jesus encountered the sicknesses, the sins, the demons, and the troubles of the masses, He already had within Him (through relationship and encounter with God) everything necessary to confront and conquer the impossible. Jesus did not need time to pray before performing miracles, because He knew beyond any doubt that the Father was backing Him completely!

David ran toward Goliath for the same reason: He knew God and He knew God was with him.

Now let's turn our focus on the battle itself:

> *Then he took his staff in his hand; and he chose for himself five smooth stones from the brook, and put them in a shepherd's bag, in a pouch which he had, and his sling was in his hand. And he drew near to the Philistine. So the Philistine came, and began drawing near to David, and the man who bore the shield went before him. And when the Philistine looked about and saw David, he disdained him, for he was only a youth, ruddy and good-looking. So the Philistine said to David, "Am I a dog, that you come to me with sticks?"*
> (1 Samuel 17:40-43)

When Goliath saw David running towards him, he despised him...and underestimated him. Big mistake! It is interesting how Goliath perceived David: the same way David's own brothers did, just a shepherd boy.

The Philistine evaluated the situation only by what he could see in the natural. His perspective was the exact opposite of David's. While Goliath was "stuck" with seeing David only as a young, handsome (pretty boy), shepherd, David looked past Goliath's armor, physical strength, and experience, and saw him defeated and destroyed.

> *And the Philistine cursed David by his gods. And the Philistine said to David, "Come to me, and I will give your flesh to the birds of the air and the beasts of the field."*
> (1 Samuel 43-44)

Bigger mistake! Goliath's "gods," by which he cursed David, could not touch David; therefore, the curse that couldn't stick on David bounced right back on Goliath. Everything the Philistine spoke against David happened to *him*!

Another fatal error on Goliath's part was to determine how the battle would end before the battle even began. The outcome of any battle is *only* determined by what happens *during* the battle.

It was now David's turn to make predictions. Every word David spoke was prophetic. It had the backing of heaven.

> *Then David said to the Philistine, "You come to me with a sword, with a spear, and with a javelin. But I come to you in the name of the LORD of hosts, the God of the armies of Israel, whom you have defied."*
> (1 Samuel 17:45)

David does not express confidence in anything that has to do with his own life, experience, or abilities. He only says, "*I come to you in the Name of the Lord of Hosts,*" and that is all it took! David was fighting in God's Name, and that Name was above every other name in heaven and on the earth.

Then the final (prophetic) blow was released:

> *This day the LORD will deliver you into my hand, and I will strike you and take your head from you.*
> (1 Samuel 17:46)

David was prophesying under the influence and power of the Holy Spirit. The outcome of the battle had already been determined, and David had seen it!

Confidence in the face of impossibilities comes from seeing what the Father is doing and hearing what He is saying.

When we see and hear what the Father has in mind, the impossible will occur. I was once in a service where a man stood at the altar with desperation all over his face. He was slouched over, and he was using a cane for support. I looked at him, closed my eyes, and saw the Father taking the cane and throwing it on the ground forcefully.

I asked the man about his suffering. The moment he told me about his ruptured disks and gave me permission to pray for him, I took his cane and threw it on the ground. I prayed a simple prayer. Within minutes, the man who could not stand without the help of his cane started jumping, walking, and even running in place. The mental image of the Father throwing down the cane gave me boldness to physically throw down the cane and the confidence to pray without inhibition.

The ability to see and hear the Father stems from a personal relationship with God. The origin of such faith and boldness is the "prayer closet."

The ability to see and hear the Father stems from a personal relationship with God. The origin of such faith and boldness is the "prayer closet."

Through his relationship with the Father, David saw what God was doing long before he stood on the battlefield facing Goliath. He had already seen Goliath on the ground with his head chopped off. He had already seen the Philistines running for their lives. The Father had already ordained for it to happen; all David had to do was faithfully execute in the natural what he had seen and sensed in the Spirit.

The next verse is very important:

"And this day I will give the carcasses of the camp of the Philistines to the birds of the air and the wild beasts of the earth, that all the earth may know that there is a God in Israel."
(1 Samuel 17:46)

David's motive was that all the nations of the earth would know that there was a living God in Israel who empowered young shepherds to topple formidable giants.

Verse 46 gives the reason for the confrontation between David and Goliath from God's perspective. David's motive for fighting Goliath was not to prove to Saul, his brothers, and all the other naysayers that he was big and strong enough to handle the Philistine super-warrior. Nor was it David's motive to gain fame, glory, acceptance, and recognition in all of Israel. David's motive was that all the nations of the earth would know that there was a living God in Israel who empowered young shepherds to topple formidable giants.

David was born and raised in the tiny town of Bethlehem, a country smaller than the state of New Jersey. Knowing what we do about David's upbringing, his family background, and his occupation as a shepherd over his father's flocks, we can assume David had always lived and operated within a small geographical radius. And yet, he tells Goliath, *"Today, you will be defeated that the whole world will know that Israel's God is the true God!"*

Why does David have "all the earth" in mind at the moment he is facing Goliath, when he hasn't traveled beyond the borders of tiny Israel? Because that is what happens when we take on the impossible – it broadens our vision, it expands our horizons, and it changes our perspectives forever!

When we run towards impossibilities we move beyond our limited scope of influence into the unlimited potential God has placed within us.

When you choose to run toward the challenges, the hardships, and the afflictions of your life, you will grow in vision and in insight, and you will begin to look beyond the limited dimensions of your own life.

When we run towards impossibilities we move beyond our limited scope of influence into the unlimited potential God has placed within us. The impossible thrusts us into our destiny, and our destiny is always bigger than anything we can comprehend or see in the natural! Our destiny was determined before the foundations of the world were

> God moves in individuals with the bigger picture in mind: the nations of the world.

laid by our Creator and Master, who is unlimited in all regards.

When we begin to take on the challenges we cannot overcome in our own natural ability, we tune into God's supernatural frequencies; they always broadcast God's perspective. God never sees just one person, one leader, one assignment, one business, one church, one government, one community, one country. God moves in individuals with the bigger picture in mind: the nations of the world.

That is why David spoke of the nations when he didn't know about them. Running to the impossible changed him for good.

Impossibility will change you, my friend, one way or the other. It will cause you to run and hide in a trench for forty days while the enemy is hurling insults against your God, or it will cause you to stand up boldly, declaring, "*I'm going to face it, I'm going to run to it, I'm going to topple it, I'm going to conquer it and I'm going to prove that my God is big!*"

How is impossibility going to change *you*?

When he stood in front of Goliath, in fact, *because* he dared to stand in front of Goliath, David's vision transcended the hills of Bethlehem, the confines of Judea, and even the borders of Israel. David no longer saw Goliath for the intimidating foe he was. David saw the testimony of Goliath's demise spreading to the nations. That is what God wanted, and David was tuned into heaven's frequency and understood the purposes of God in this confrontation.

There was one more motive behind David's brave charge:

> *"Then all this assembly shall know that the LORD does not save with sword and spear; for the battle is the LORD's, and He will give you into our hands."*
> (1 Samuel 17:47)

Defeating Goliath would also bring a much-needed shift in the mindset and attitude of the Israelites, especially those who were fighting for Saul at the Valley of Elam. For forty days, and most likely for much longer than that, Israel had developed a defeatist mentality.

David, seeing situations from God's perspective, declared that Goliath's destruction would cause Israel to remember that their battle was God's battle, and if they trusted Him and ran to the battle, they would always win!

When you commit your life to Jesus Christ and recognize Him as your Lord and Savior, Israel's God becomes your God. Your battles are then *His* battles, because you belong to Him through Christ.

The circumstances of your life may have brought you to conclusions that do not reflect the godly purposes and calling that reside within you. Continual financial pressures may have led you to believe you can never prosper in life. Pain and disease in your body may have broken down your faith and hope for healing. You may have even believed the lie that *God brought on the sickness and suffering, in order to build character in you.*

Moreover, traumas, failures, or setbacks throughout your life may have caused you to be fearful about taking initiative or launching out to unfamiliar areas. If these or any other circumstances have robbed you of your confidence and courage to face impossibilities, you are a great candidate for breakthrough.

I encourage you to pray the following prayer out loud. Let us believe together that God will demonstrate His power and His glory in your life. May God answer our prayer and bring a life-transforming mindset shift!

Heavenly Father,

I recognize that issues I have been dealing with have negatively affected my faith. I have lost some of my hope in the victory that Jesus secured when He died for me on the cross. The challenges and problems of my life have hindered me from accepting your love and trusting in your grace. I need a breakthrough—I need *You*!

I ask you, Father, to move powerfully in my life and change me. Strengthen my heart, increase my faith, and enlighten the eyes of my understanding. Help me always to remember that I am yours through Jesus. Help me not to see my struggles as dead ends, but as on-ramps to the highway of my destiny.

Help me to see every impossibility as an opportunity for more glory and honor to be ascribed to your Name. Quicken me to remember that there is nothing, absolutely nothing, I face that you cannot turn around to benefit me and use for my advancement.

Let your presence fill my heart with confidence and joy.

In Jesus Name,

Amen

CHAPTER 7

TOPPLING THE IMPOSSIBLE

So it was, when the Philistine arose and came and drew near to meet David that David hurried and ran toward the army to meet the Philistine.
(1 Samuel 17:48)

Someone observing the events at the Valley of Elam and evaluating the scenario strictly by appearance could easily have asked, "How could David run towards as formidable an opponent as Goliath?" In the natural, David did not look capable of fighting Goliath, much less defeating him.

In light of what we now know about David, and especially his relationship with God, I pose the question, "How could he *not* run?"

Every step David took towards the Philistine warrior brought him closer to the victory, closer to his destiny, and closer to being established as a mighty man of God. In addition, as we saw earlier, every step towards Goliath was another step *away* from David's critics and the skeptics who told him he could not succeed. Moreover, through his prophetic insight, David had already seen Goliath on the ground with his head chopped off! David knew God had already granted him the victory. How could he not run?

Once you know that God is with you, and that the resources of heaven are available to you through Christ; once you know that the victory is guaranteed because you've seen what the Father is doing; once you've recognized that your five smooth stones are more accurate than a smart bomb, the only thing left to do is run towards the impossibility up ahead. The quicker the better!

The next time the phone rings and there is an impossibility on the other end; the next time you open up the mailbox and there is an impossibility in an envelope; the next time you hear the report that they are laying off people at your company; the next time you hear such things, start running, not away from the impending challenges, but right to them!

> *Then David put his hand in his bag and took out a stone; and he slung it and struck the Philistine in his forehead, so that the stone sank into his forehead, and he fell on his face to the earth. So David prevailed over the Philistine with a sling and a stone, and struck the Philistine and killed him. But there was no sword in the hand of David. Therefore David ran and stood over the Philistine, took his sword and drew it out of its sheath and killed him, and cut off his head with it.*
> (1 Samuel 17: 49-51)

I love these verses because they clearly point out that David did not have a great arsenal at his disposal, but he won anyway! David's God fought *for* him and *through* him.

We cannot do God's part. However, God will only do His part if we are faithful to do ours first. He wants to see us stepping out in faith, obeying the voice of the Spirit within us, and taking steps towards impossibilities.

> I believe David would have toppled Goliath whether he was accurate with a slingshot or not.

I believe David would have toppled Goliath whether he was accurate with a slingshot or not. I used to preach that, "*David practiced with his slingshot out in the fields while tending sheep – he was a good shot because he practiced!*"

We cannot know whether or not David actually practiced. However, we do know that David could not have done what he did without God! He said, "*God will deliver you Goliath into my hands today.*" God directed that stone into Goliath's temple. I believe Jehovah said something like this, "*David, you have the heart, the willpower, and the backing of heaven. You've proven your courage and faith by running to the impossible! Hurl that stone and watch what I'll do!*"

There is a part, my friend, that God has done for you. He sent His Son to die for you. He watched his only begotten Son suffer in ways we cannot fully comprehend in the natural. God watched people beat Jesus' head with staffs. They put a crown of thorns on His head and pressed it down until blood flowed freely.

The Roman soldiers put a purple robe on Christ's back and mocked Him, saying, "*Hail the King of the Jews.*" They punched him, slapped him, pulled his hair, and spat on Him. You would never endure even a few moments of such abuse against your own child. You would intervene. God however, allowed the agony to continue. He did it for us, you and me!

Jesus bore all the physical pain and verbal stabs; He endured the lashes on His back. Isaiah 53 states that He was unrecognizable. He hung on the cross, He bled on the cross and they drove nails through His hands and feet. His executioners would not even give Him some water to drink when He asked for it; instead they gave Him vinegar! That is the part God had in redeeming mankind: He sacrificed His Son for us.

Jesus was placed in a tomb for three days and on the third day the Spirit of the Living God, the same Spirit that lives in you and me, raised Christ from the dead. His resurrection was the finishing punch against hell, death, and the grave. Jesus rose victorious!

Jesus did His part. He came to earth, lived a sinless life, poured His life and anointing into His disciples, suffered the horrors of the cross, died and rose again. Jesus did His part. Our part is to believe in Him, accept His gift of grace, and walk in the newness of life that the Father made available to us by His grace.

When the giant came down, David took the sword. The Word says, *"But David did not have a sword."* Soldiers didn't go to battle without a sword! The record of the incident emphasizes that David did not have a sword so that David would always remember, and so that you and I would know, that David toppled Goliath without using a weapon of war, because God did His part and gave David a supernatural victory!

"But David did not have a sword."

May God etch into your spirit the eternal principle that emanates from this verse! It is indeed not by might, nor by power, but by the Spirit of the Living God that all giants are defeated and all impossibilities are conquered.

By the grace and power of our God, by God doing His part, as we do ours, we attain the victory—even with a slingshot. May we never forget that!

May we never forget the numerous times that God gave us unlikely victories through unconventional means. May we never forget we are fighting

His battle, and that we will prevail over our enemy. Jesus already rose victorious, once and for all!

CHAPTER 8

THE REWARD

When we face impossibilities, we naturally run *from* them. No one walks through life looking for Goliaths to fight. We prefer the easy assignments, the paths of least resistance. Facing Goliath-sized challenges takes us out of our comfort zones and increases the possibility for failure.

So far we have been learning that when we actually face our fears and ask the Lord to intervene, we enter into the process of conquering impossibilities. Through that process we grow in love, we grow in faith, and we grow in favor with the Lord. Most importantly, we learn more about the nature and ways of our God — we grow in our knowledge of Him!

As God repeatedly strengthens our hearts and helps us to overcome our challenges, our perception of the impossible changes. We no longer view the "hard stuff" as impassable walls or dead ends; instead, we view impossibilities as opportunities for increased understanding and revelation of the goodness and blessings of our God, as they are embodied in our Savior, Jesus Christ.

Through the encounters we have with the Lord while tackling impossibilities, we learn to embrace the impossibilities we once ran from, because the process of confronting them brings us closer to God. Great rewards are on the other sides of the mountains that we dare to climb.

In the last two chapters we will discuss the benefits God's faithful and obedient servants receive as a result of running to the impossible.

David's victory over Goliath encouraged Saul and his men to rise up and fight against the Philistines.

> *Now the men of Israel and Judah arose and shouted, and pursued the Philistines as far as the entrance of the valley and to the gates of Ekron. And the wounded of the Philistines fell along the road to Shaaraim, even as far as Gath and Ekron. Then the children of Israel returned from chasing the Philistines, and they plundered their tents.*
> (1 Samuel 17:52-53)

Once the battle was over and Israel's victory had been secured, Saul sent for David.

*Then, as David returned from the
slaughter of the Philistine, Abner took
him and brought him before Saul with
the head of the Philistine in his hand.*
(1 Samuel 17:57)

I love this! Every lingering trace of the Green Beret within me is fully satisfied with the divine justice proclaimed through this verse! David walked in to see the king who had told him he could not kill Goliath, *with* the head of Goliath in his hand!

> Watch how quickly some of the individuals who initially criticize and oppose you, will line up in your corner *after* you conquer impossibilities

Isn't it interesting that the skeptics and critics, who did their best to hinder David from pursuing the impossible, were so quick to set up a "meet-and-greet" for the new national hero? Watch how quickly some of the individuals who initially criticize and oppose you, will line up in your corner *after* you conquer impossibilities and prove you were right for trying.

Saul talked to David, asked him about his family background, and then offered David a job as an officer in the king's army.

> *So David went out wherever Saul sent
> him, and behaved wisely. And Saul set
> him over the men of war, and he was ac-*

cepted in the sight of all the people and also in the sight of Saul's servants.
(1 Samuel 18:5-7)

How swiftly things change. One moment David was too small and weak in Saul's eyes to fight Goliath. Within a few hours, Saul placed David in leadership over men of war. I only hope David's brothers and the rest of the soldiers who spoke against David at the Valley of Elam, were placed under David's command.

What awaits the men and women of God, who like David, dare to run to the impossible, and by God's grace are able to overcome? Promotion!

Promotion to greater awareness of God's nature and our identity in Him. Promotion to new levels of understanding and revelation. Promotion to greater influence, prominence, and authority.

It is important to note that there are breakthroughs and blessings which God releases into our lives, *only* after we demonstrate courage and faith in the face of seemingly insurmountable problems.

When I first arrived at Old Saybrook as the new pastor of Valley Shore Assembly of God, I had a strong burden to see the church parking lot enlarged, paved, and lit. The existing dirt, gravel, and few sections of asphalt were by no means adequate for parking. Among my greatest concerns was the possibility that it might rain or snow on a Sunday morning, forcing people to tread through puddles and mud to enter the building.

The absence of outside lighting added to my discontent. On a dark night, it was almost impossible to locate the church from the street. In addition, it was unsafe and uncomfortable for folks walking out of the church to their cars after evening services. We desperately needed to pave and light our parking lot!

I remember vividly the day I stood at the front corner of the property looking towards the church and thinking about the magnitude of the project ahead of us. The church finances were nowhere near the level they needed to be for us to undertake such a project. We had no savings to speak of. Neither did we have an adequate surplus at the end of each month. Moreover, since this was my first pastorate, I had no experience regarding the process I would have to follow to accomplish this task. On the day I scanned the dirt and gravel parking lot from the edge of the property, I was facing the impossible.

When I began to commit this need to the Lord in prayer, I found the courage to take the first step towards the mountain. I stood before the congregation on a Sunday morning and I encouraged everyone to give above and beyond tithes and offerings towards the paving of our parking lot. Though I boldly declared that the project would be completed within one year, debt free, I did not say anything about lighting.

Within a few weeks I experienced my break-through. A family in our church handed me two checks. One check was for a quarter of the esti-mated amount for the paving project; the other was for the entire cost of outside lighting, and....a new sign!

The generosity and obedience of the family was overwhelming. This was the first time I had received such large donations. Accompanying these gifts was the affirmation from God that He honors those who honor Him by daring to take on impossible tasks. Others followed the family's ex-ample. Within a few months we had more than half of what was needed for the paving.

Our district, recognizing the effort of the church towards the project, graciously provided a large sum to expedite the fundraising. Within six months from the time we started giving towards the paving of the parking lot, we began the work. Within one year, the paving was completed, out-side lights were installed, and the church featured a beautiful new sign.

Better yet, the spirit of generosity spread throughout the congregation. We agreed to sup-port more missionaries; we sowed into the com-munity through benevolence; we began to dream about building a new sanctuary debt-free (our current impossibility). It was as though the floodgates of vision had opened wide.

I am fully convinced the catalyst for the Lord's provision for our immediate need, as well as the broadening of our spiritual horizons that followed, was our determination to take the first step towards the impossible.

When we allow the process of overcoming impossibilities to bring us to a place of greater dependence on the grace, love, and power of our Heavenly Father; when running to the impossible brings us into life-changing encounters with Him, we come to the other side of the mountain and find promotion to new levels of faith and glory.

The children of Israel could not get to the Promised Land from slavery unless they moved *out* of Egypt and *towards* the impossibilities of crossing the Red Sea and living in the wilderness for forty years. Next, they had to cross over into Canaan. That could only happen by crossing the waters of the Jordan River. God instructed Joshua, *"Have your people, your priests, your elders and the heads of the tribes stand in the water."* The breakthrough came after God's people first made a move towards the impossible.

Once *into* Canaan, the Israelites had to take possession of the land by confronting one impossibility after another. The most notable one was Jericho. The city was a mighty stronghold, protected

On the other side of our impossibilities, we will find promotion.

from invaders by huge walls. In order for Jericho's walls to come down, Joshua and his people had to march around the city for seven days, thirteen times in all!

Some of the breakthroughs you and I have been praying for and so desperately need, will not come until we find the courage to confront obstacles, problems, and challenges. When we stop avoiding the battle, but instead run *to* the battle, heaven's backing will assure us of the victory, and on the other side of our impossibilities, we will find promotion.

The promotion I speak of is not one that comes from man. The promotion comes from God.

We will examine David's promotion into higher realms of authority and significance in God's Kingdom in a moment. First, let us look at divinely orchestrated promotion as evidenced in the life of another impossibility-crusher, Daniel.

We meet Daniel in the first chapter of the book of Daniel as a young man; by the end of the book, he is old. Daniel started as a mere slave, but he eventually became one of the most influential men in the world.

Daniel was a captive of the Chaldeans. The Babylonians led Daniel along with a few other prominent Jewish youth to the capital, Susa, and housed him in the palace. These children were being prepared to be enchanters, magicians, astrologers, and servants of the king, whose name was Nebuchadnezzar; thus, they were raised with care and given rich food.

While in that state of captivity, Daniel faced an impossibility. In fact, by the time of his passing, Daniel had dealt with impossibilities for all of the four kings he served. There's an impossibility for you—four heathen emperors, rulers of the largest empires of that day. If you think you have a tough boss, or if you resent working in an ungodly environment, be encouraged by Daniel, who was able to serve *and influence* not just one or two, but all four heathen kings.

How did Daniel influence these men? By conquering the impossible through the help and grace of Jehovah.

The first impossibility was to interpret Nebuchadnezzar's troublesome dream. Daniel heard about the dream when he became aware that the king had ordered the deaths of all the magicians, enchanters, and wise men of the land. The king had had a dream they could not interpret.

When the king had a bad dream and asked for interpretation, the wise men et al said, *"Tell us the dream and we'll give you the interpretation."* Anybody can come up with an interpretation that sounds good if he knows the dream! That's what the magicians and company had been doing all along! Yet, this time, Nebuchadnezzar demanded that they come up with both the dream and the interpretation.

Obviously, the king's wise men were stuck. They could produce neither the dream nor the interpretation, because there was no divine power revealing to them the secrets of another man's heart. Their insight had been coming from the powers of the kingdom of darkness; those powers extend just so far.

Therefore, the king ordered the execution of the wise men and their entire households. Daniel caught wind of the king's order, and realized his life was also in jeopardy, for he was being groomed to serve the king as a wise man.

> *He asked the king's officer, "Why did the king issue such a harsh decree?" Arioch then explained the matter to Daniel. At this, Daniel went in to the king and asked for time, so that he might interpret the dream for him.*
> (Daniel 1:15–16)

Did you get that? Daniel "went in to the king." He moved towards the impossibility, not around it, and not away from it. Basically, here's what Daniel told the king. *"I will have the interpretation! God is going to give it to me!"* He was running toward the impossible, just as David had done. Different men, different times, different kingdoms, and different impossibilities, but the same concept: confronting the impossible with faith in God!

> *Then Daniel returned to his house and explained the matter to his friends Hananiah, Mishael and Azariah. (We know them as Shadrach, Meschach, and Abednigo.) He urged them to plead for mercy from the God of heaven concerning this mystery, so that he and his friends might not be executed with the rest of the wise men of Babylon. During the night the mystery was revealed to Daniel in a vision.*
> (Daniel 1:17 – 19)

Daniel had an encounter with God through a vision, and the Lord gave Daniel the interpretation.

> *Then King Nebuchadnezzar fell on his face, prostrate before Daniel, and commanded that they should present an offering and incense to him. The king answered Daniel, and said, "Truly your God is the God of gods, the Lord of kings, and a revealer of secrets, since you could reveal this secret." Then the king promoted Daniel and gave him many great gifts; and he made him ruler over the whole*

province of Babylon and chief adminis-
trator over all the wise men of Babylon.
(Daniel 1:46)

Promotion came after Daniel conquered the impossibility of interpreting the dream.

A few years later, Daniel had a similar promotion offered by Nebuchadnezzar's successor, Belshazzar.

Belshazzar held a huge banquet at the palace in Babylon. He invited everyone who was important and proceeded to entertain his guests by offering them the opportunity to drink from the sacred vessels which had been taken out of the temple of God in Jerusalem by Nebuchadnezzar many years earlier.

While everyone was enjoying the drinking extravaganza, suddenly a disconnected hand appeared and started writing on the wall. That will kill a party quickly! The Bible says Belshazzar's knees knocked together from fear, and his legs could not bear the weight of the rest of his body. Though Belshazzar did not have a relationship with the God who was behind the writing on the wall, he knew enough *about* Him to know he had messed with the wrong Deity!

Belshazzar called Daniel to help solve the riddle.

I have heard of you that you can give interpretations and explain enigmas. Now if you can read the writing and make known to me its interpretation, you shall be clothed with purple and have a chain of gold around your neck and shall be the third ruler in the kingdom.
(Daniel 5:16)

Beware! The world will offer material goods in return for the anointing. When Elisha told Naaman to go dip into the water and be healed, what happened when Naaman came out of the water healed? He said, *"What great gifts can I give to you?"* Elisha replied, *"Is this time to receive gifts?"* (I wish the church would learn that!)

What was Belshazzar offering Daniel in return for his services? Promotion. I like Daniel's response, *"Keep your gifts."*

This is the interpretation of each word. MENE: God has numbered your kingdom, and finished it; TEKEK: You have been weighed in the balances, and found wanting; PERES: Your kingdom has been divided, and given to the Medes and Persians.
(Daniel 5:26)

That was by no means a favorable word for the Babylonian king. In essence, David proclaimed, "Belshazzar, you're done!" Yet, because Belshazzar recognized it was the Word of the Lord coming through Daniel, the king still promoted Daniel.

> *Then Belshazzar gave the command, and they clothed Daniel with purple and put a chain of gold around his neck, and made a proclamation concerning him that he should be the third ruler in the kingdom.*
> (Daniel 5:29)

Remember, promotion on the other side of impossibilities ultimately comes from God. God was behind Daniel's promotion.

Within hours after Belshazzar appointed Daniel to be third ruler in the kingdom, the Persians broke into the capital, took command of the city, and overtook the Babylonian empire. Because Daniel had already been appointed, the Persians left him at his post. Therefore, Daniel remained in a position where he would exert godly influence on the next ruler, Darius.

Let's see what happens when Darius is the king.

> *And the king gave the command, and they brought those men who had accused Daniel, and they cast them into the den of lions.*
> (Daniel 6:16)

Daniel had been thrown into the lions' den because of a conspiracy against him. The princes were jealous of his becoming third in the kingdom and then being promoted to be their overseer. They tricked the king into making a decree that they knew would incriminate Daniel, and they tried to destroy him.

The king is forced by the decree to throw Daniel into the lions' den, but God caused the mouths of the lions to be shut by the power of an angel, and Daniel conquered that impossibility of hungry lions as well. The king comes back to the den worried and asks *"Daniel, are you still alive, did your God protect you?"* Daniel answers, *"I'm fine!"*

The king brings Daniel out and turns his attention to the false accusers. They had caused Daniel to be cast into the den of lions, but now the king takes the princes and throws *them* in!

The Lord is always going to turn the tables on the devil. When satan oppresses you, when he torments you and bothers you, because you are in Christ, because He loves you, and because you are called according to His purpose, *God works all things for good!* There's going to be a reversal – not of fortune, but of your destiny!

> *And the king gave the command, and they brought those men who had accused Daniel, and they cast them into the den of lions – them, their children, and their wives; and the lions overpowered them,*

*and broke all their bones in pieces before
they ever came to the bottom of the den.*
(Daniel 6:24)

Why? Because the lions had been hungry and
frustrated because they couldn't eat Daniel all
night!

> *Then King Darius wrote:*
> *To all peoples, nations, and languages
> that dwell in all the earth: Peace be mul-
> tiplied to you. I make a decree that in
> every dominion of my kingdom men
> must tremble and fear before the God of
> Daniel. For He is the living God, and
> steadfast forever; His kingdom is the one
> which shall not be destroyed,*
> *and His dominion shall endure to the
> end. He delivers and rescues, And He
> works signs and wonders In heaven and
> on earth, Who has delivered Daniel from
> the power of the lions.*
>
> *So this Daniel prospered in the reign of
> Darius and in the reign of Cyrus the
> Persian.*
> (Daniel 6:25-28)

Daniel served four different kings. Under each
one, Daniel faced, confronted, and with God's
help, conquered the impossible. Consequently,
Daniel was promoted to great prominence and influence!

When people see us, and our God flowing through us, they will want to promote us to greater prominence. We may get pay raises, added benefits, and/or our own offices. We need to be cautious because prominence and all the perks associated with it can distract us from exercising the influence God gives us as the result of our victories.

> Influence is more important than prominence. We must never be affected by prominence in a way that will diminish our influence.

Influence is more important than prominence. We must never be affected by prominence in a way that will diminish our influence. We must be stewards of prominence to gain more influence.

Influence comes when the grace and the power of the living God, the God of the Bible, is demonstrated through our lives! That grace and power is greatly enhanced when we confront impossibilities with faith and overcome them by the grace of God.

Whenever we confront and conquer impossibilities, some heads will undoubtedly turn in our direction. What we do when the attention is drawn to us, is critical. Being celebrated, recognized, and put on pedestals will only last for a little while; eventually, we will come back down to earth. If we

> Every time Daniel demonstrated the supernatural power of his God to deliver him...God promoted Daniel to another realm of influence.

choose to direct the attention to the Lord, which is where it *should* go, our influence and (Kingdom) notoriety will grow.

Every time Daniel demonstrated the supernatural power of his God to deliver him from the impossibilities he faced, God promoted Daniel to another realm of influence. Out of those four kings, three of them made a confession of faith in Daniel's God. At least two issued decrees that all the people in their empires must worship the God of Daniel!

Just as several kings had promoted Daniel, Saul promoted David after seeing him kill Goliath. David was promoted because he could conquer the impossibilities Saul was afraid to deal with. Saul basically hired David to do his dirty work. *"Let David go out and risk his life killing Philistines!"*

Saul had his agenda, and God had His! Saul promoted David to better his own position as king and as "commander in chief" of Israel's armies. God promoted David to better David's position.

God's purpose for David transcended Saul's political and selfish motives. Through the various roles David served in Saul's courts, God was grooming David, not just to be a giant killer, an officer, or a personal worship leader, but also to be the next king!

Moreover, God was aligning David's life with the prophesies which stated that the line of David would bring forth, not only future kings of Israel, but also the King of Kings and the Lord of Lords! From the line of David would come the Christ, the Messiah, Jesus our Lord!

> *And in that day there shall be a Root of Jesse, who shall stand as a banner to the people. For the Gentiles shall seek Him, And His resting place shall be glorious.*
> (Isaiah 11:10)

> *Now in the sixth month the angel Gabriel was sent by God to a city of Galilee named Nazareth, to a virgin betrothed to a man whose name was Joseph, of the house of David. The virgin's name was Mary.*
> (Luke 1:26-27)

> *Jesus Christ our Lord, who was born of the seed of David according to the flesh.*
> (Romans 1:3)

David's promotion which followed his running to the battle against Goliath ultimately pointed to God's desire to bring through David's line His Son, Jesus, the Savior of the world. Even though the events we are exploring in this incident in David's life occurred hundreds of years before the coming of Christ, they are still intricately connected to God's marvelous plan of salvation.

God's plan includes you, my friend. He loves you so much, that He sent His Son to die for you.

Before you turn to the concluding chapter of this book, I encourage you to take inventory of your heart. If you have never asked Jesus Christ to be your Lord and Savior, or if through your choices in life, you find yourself to be distant from God, I urge you to take a few moments to turn the reins of your life over to the Lord.

Join me in this prayer:

Heavenly Father, I know that I am far from you right now — I need a Savior! I recognize and confess my sins and shortcomings before You. Please forgive me, Father, and restore my life.

I accept the sacrifice of Your Son Jesus. I believe Jesus died so I would not have to pay the penalty for my sins. I believe that when Jesus rose from the grave, He defeated sin and death once and for all.

I receive your forgiveness, Father, and I submit to Your will and to Your ways. I trust You with every aspect of my life. I ask You to guide me, direct me, and use me for Your glory.

Thank You for the newness of life and purpose You bring to me through Jesus.

I love You.

In Jesus Name,

Amen.

If you prayed this prayer for the first time or if you recommitted your life to Christ, you have just made the greatest decision of your life!

Welcome to the Kingdom of God! I am honored to be your brother in Christ and to serve our Savior alongside you!

CHAPTER 9

PERKS OF PROMOTION

*S*o David went out wherever Saul sent him, and behaved wisely. And Saul set him over the men of war, and he was accepted in the sight of all the people and also in the sight of Saul's servants. Now it had happened as they were coming home, when David was returning from the slaughter of the Philistine, that the women had come out of all the cities of Israel, singing and dancing, to meet King Saul, with tambourines, with joy, and with musical instruments. So the women sang as they danced, and said:

'Saul has slain his thousands,
and David his ten thousands.'
(1 Samuel 18:5-7)

When David defeated Goliath, he walked into Saul's tent with the head of Goliath as a trophy! This "trophy" represented David's faith in God, the favor and blessing of the Lord on David's life, and the divine grace by which David was able to overcome the giant. Consequently, Saul promoted David.

David's promotion as an officer in Saul's army was initiated by an earthly king, but ultimately, it was a promotion from God. Working through the systems and the infrastructure of Saul's kingdom and Israel's military, God was working to move David from the sheepfold to the palace, to transform David from a shepherd to a king.

God's promotions differ from the promotions that come from man.

God's promotions differ from the promotions that come from man. When people are promoted by their employers, the promotion changes their external circumstances. They are given more authority, they assume greater responsibility, they receive an increase in pay, and they are likely to obtain various new benefits.

Perhaps you have been the recipient of such a promotion. Individuals who were once your superiors may now be reporting to you. You may have a new and improved workstation, your own phone line, or your own office with a swivel chair and a large window with a view. You may even have a company vehicle or an expense account that allows you to take people out to lunch. Regardless of the specific details in your case, the fact is, promotion changes your external circumstances.

As wonderful as that kind of promotion may be, it does not compare with the promotions God gives. *His* promotions do not only change the external circumstances of life, they also change us within, transforming us from the inside out. Through His promotion, God deposits in us the attributes that change the very environments in which we operate. We see this principle in effect with David.

> *So David went out wherever Saul sent him and behaved wisely. And Saul set him over the men of war.*
> (1 Samuel 18:5)

Obedience, loyalty, faithfulness, submission to authority – those are character qualities that were already present in David's life. After the promotion came, those qualities shot to another level.

It says David *"behaved wisely."* David's promotion was accompanied with a much-needed increase in wisdom, discernment, and understanding. David was no longer just responsible for sheep on a hillside in Bethlehem; he was in charge of soldiers who would protect and advance Israel. His growth in wisdom would ultimately enable David to rule the nation.

Moreover, David increased in authority. His views and his directives carried weight among God's people because the Lord was instilling in David the qualities essential for dominion.

The life of Jesus serves as a perfect illustration of divine authority at work. When Jesus preached, He preached not as the scribes but He preached with authority (see Matthew 7:29, Mark 1:22.) When Jesus said, "*Stand up!*" somebody whose physical condition prohibited such activity, would immediately stand. When the Lord commanded demons to leave the man by the graveyard of Gadara and go into pigs, the demons obeyed Jesus and did exactly as He said. Even the forces of nature obeyed Him.

> Amazing things happen in and through us when divine authority increases in our lives.

Every miracle, healing, deliverance, and manifestation of God's glory by Jesus came after He spoke into that specific situation with God-given authority. Divine authority backed up everything Jesus proclaimed. Amazing things happen in and through us when divine authority increases in our lives.

Another perk to David's God-ordained promotion was favor:

> *...and he was accepted in the sight of all the people and also in the sight of Saul's servants.*
> (1 Samuel 18:5)

As David's ministry and success continued to increase, people grew to love and respect him. The people he worked with, those who served under him, the leadership over him, and all who were around him, loved and honored David. All except one....King Saul.

Saul perceived David's charismatic personality and his great exploits as a threat to his own interests as king. The success and favor David enjoyed offended King Saul.

> *Now it had happened as they were coming home, when David was returning from the slaughter of the Philistine, that the women had come out of all the cities of Israel, singing and dancing, to meet King Saul, with tambourines, with joy, and with musical instruments. So the women sang as they danced, and said:*
> *'Saul has slain his thousands,*
> *and David his ten thousands.'*
> (1 Samuel 18:6-7)

When the women of Israel came out en masse to greet Saul's army and celebrate the victory, they already knew of David's part in the battle. Thus, they honored David with their song. The women were not out of line. They were by no means dishonoring Saul, nor were they minimizing the king's accomplishments. Saul had slain his thousands, but David, in this particular instance, had slain his tens of thousands!

If Saul had cultivated the heart of a leader who wanted those that were under him to grow and even outdo him, he would have joined in the praise of David, as he *should* have. But Saul's heart was not right, and neither was his response:

> *Now Saul was afraid of David, because the LORD was with him, but had departed from Saul. Therefore Saul removed him from his presence, and made him his captain over a thousand; and he went out and came in before the people.*
> (1 Samuel 18:13)

When Saul heard the women's song, he became jealous and fearful of David. Saul came under the influence of a demonic spirit, which ultimately put Saul in the grip of the enemy.

It is clear from the biblical account that Saul made David captain over a thousand in hopes that David would get killed in battle. Not only did David not get killed, he also thrived in that position.

> *And David behaved wisely in all his ways, and the LORD was with him.*
> (1 Samuel 18:14)

David responded to all of Saul's antics with honor and wisdom; consequently, David achieved more success and gained more favor from all who were watching.

Therefore, when Saul saw that he be-
haved very wisely, he was afraid of him.
But all Israel and Judah loved David, be-
cause he went out and came in before
them.
(1 Samuel 18:15)

With time, Saul's fear and insecurity festered into outright bitterness and hatred. Saul despised David and wanted him dead. Being influenced by forces from the kingdom of darkness, Saul launched an attempt to kill David. When it failed, he tried again, and again, and again—twenty-one attempts in all.

Though some of Saul's campaigns to eliminate David were prepared and executed well, they were not successful. Part of the reason for Saul's failure was David's sharp mind and his elusiveness; however, there was another significant factor contributing to David's survival: God's protection.

God's promotion comes with God's protection, a Heavenly covering to ensure that His people and His plan for them will come to pass. When you enter that perfect will of God, and you selflessly and wholeheartedly pursue His will for your life, and especially when you dare to run towards impossibilities, you get locked into God's Witness Protection Program. He becomes your strong tower and He covers you under the shadow of His wing!

Years ago, while my wife and I were serving as youth leaders, we became involved with the summer camps for the children and youth of our district. At the first camp we attended, we met a man who had once served in the Coast Guard as a sniper at President George Bush's residence in Kennebunkport, Maine.

Since I had served as a sniper in the Cyprus Special Forces, I quickly seized the opportunity to approach this man and strike up conversation with him. We had some great long talks during that week of camp.

One of the most remarkable facts this former sniper shared concerned the protective action that took place behind the scenes every time the President decided to come out of the residence. The incident that stood out in my mind was when the President went fishing with his grandson.

The President would walk outside with his grandson, fishing rods in hand. With the exception of a few secret service agents sparsely scattered across the lawn, all one could see was the President and his grandson walking leisurely towards the President's boat—a beautiful picture.

Here's what was happening in the background:

In the trees or behind bushes were fully armed members of the coast guard—snipers like my friend—making sure nobody was around who might want to harm the President. Under the boat were divers who were checking to make sure there was nothing or no one harmful underwater. Secret Service agents had already performed a thorough safety inspection of the various compartments of the boat.

Once the President and his guest boarded the boat and were under way, the boat would be watched from primarily unseen Coast Guard vessels that were fully prepared to move in if necessary. Moreover, F16 fighter jets were ready to take off from a nearby air base at a moment's notice.

My friend said, *"There was a large radius around the President's boat, where nobody could enter who had no business being there."* Yet, *"all the layers of protection around the President were invisible to him and his grandson"*!

Likewise, God's angels—"Heaven's Secret Service"—watch over you and me. We get up in the morning, get dressed, head out the door, and drive to work. By all appearances, we are alone in our cars; yet, invisible agents secure our protection.

> *Because you have made the LORD, who*
> *is my refuge,*
> *Even the Most High, your dwelling*
> *place, no evil shall befall you,*
> *Nor shall any plague come near your*
> *dwelling; For He shall give His angels*

*charge over you, To keep you in all your
ways.
In their hands they shall bear you up,
lest you dash your foot against a stone.*
(Psalm 91:9-12)

Think about how closely and carefully we
watch over our children as they play in the yard or
at the park. As the children play with their friends
and enjoy all the toys and rides available, they
have no idea how well supervised they are and
how we, their parents, are prepared to intervene in
a heartbeat, if necessary.

People would have to be crazy to come near
your children, your grandchildren, or any other
loved one to try to harm them when you are watching over them. Imagine how God feels towards
you, especially when He births within you purpose
and destiny for the advancement of His Kingdom.
Imagine how He feels when anyone tries to thwart
His plan for your life. Imagine how *He* feels!

The demonic spirit that possessed King Saul
convinced Saul to kill David. Yet Saul failed every
time he tried to lay a hand on David, because God
had ordained that David would be the king of
Israel, the very leader who would *replace* Saul. Saul
disqualified himself by the way he acted, and God
said, *"It's going to go to David."*

In one of the instances when David was running for his life, David sought refuge in a town

called Nob. That was the city where all the priests lived with their families, with their children, and their livestock.

Upon his arrival at Nob, David approached the high priest whose name was Ahimelech. The high priest, operating under the assumption that David was still working for Saul, helped him by giving him food to eat and the sword of Goliath, which happened to be in the temple as a war relic.

Another man happened to be at Nob that day, Doeg the Edomite, who saw David speaking with Ahimelech. Doeg, seeking to gain the favor of the king, ran to Saul with a full report of what he had witnessed. Then Saul, who by that point was paranoid to the point of insanity, marched to Nob and called in Ahimelech and all the priests for questioning.

Though Ahimelech spoke truthfully about his ignorance of the falling out between David and Saul, the king accused the high priest of treason and betrayal, and condemned him and all the others for having helped the fugitive, David.

> *Then the king said to the guards who stood about him, "Turn and kill the priests of the LORD, because their hand also is with David, and because they knew when he fled and did not tell it to me." But the servants of the king would not lift their hands to strike the priests of*

*the LORD. And the king said to Doeg,
"You turn and kill the priests!" So Doeg
the Edomite turned and struck the
priests, and killed on that day eighty-five
men who wore a linen ephod. Also Nob,
the city of the priests, he struck with the
edge of the sword, both men and women,
children and nursing infants, oxen and
donkeys and sheep – with the edge of the
sword.* (1 Samuel 22:17-20)

Can you imagine that? Saul ordered the execution of the priests and the annihilation of their entire families. Some of the worst dictators who have
lived on this planet did not do as badly as Saul did
that day.

*Now one of the sons of Ahimelech the
son of Ahitub, named Abiathar, escaped
and fled after David. And Abiathar told
David that Saul had killed the LORD's
priests. So David said to Abiathar, "I
knew that day, when Doeg the Edomite
was there, that he would surely tell Saul.
I have caused the death of all the persons
of your father's house. Stay with me; do
not fear. For he who seeks my life seeks
your life, but with me you shall be safe."*
(1 Samuel 22:17-23)

The only survivor, the only person who sur-
vived the annihilation of Nob, left that scene of
death, horror, and despair, and he went straight to
David. I must admit this baffled me.

Though David was by no means responsible for Saul's actions, David's appearance at Nob was the catalyst for the massacre. The implication that the priests had sided with David cost them and the entire town their lives. They were wiped out because of Saul's hatred of David, yet the only survivor of the onslaught ran *to* David.

What seems even more bizarre than Abiathar's willingness to seek sanctuary with David, was David's response:

"I am responsible for the death of your father's whole family. Stay with me; don't be afraid; the man who is seeking your life is seeking mine also. You will be safe with me."

How could David have made such a statement when an entire population had just been destroyed because of him?

Here's why – because David was still breathing. He was still alive; and the reason for David's survival was God's protection. No one would lay a finger on David; no weapon formed against him would prosper, because God had determined that David would be the next king. Whatever comes from the mouth of God will come to pass. When a door is opened by God, no man can shut it.

There could have been fifteen Sauls on the prowl, there could have been three million soldiers out to capture David, and there could be a nuclear holocaust in the entire gion, but David would survive. God had spoken it—David would be the next king!

Let it sink deep into your spirit, friend. Let the Word of the Living God and David's story enlighten your understanding to get a hold of how wonderful a Father God is to you. He watches over you day and night. He thinks good thoughts and has good plans for your life. If God be for you, who can be against you?! He is yours and you are His, forever!

> [God] watches over you day and night. He thinks good thoughts and has good plans for your life.

EPILOGUE

Cyprus Special Forces training included an annual twenty-five mile march. We affectionately referred to it as the *"Long Hike."* Each soldier carried all the gear necessary for battle, a weight of approximately forty-five pounds. We marched through the night in unfamiliar territory and ended at a shooting range, where each of us was expected to land, without a scope, a minimum of eight out of ten rounds through standard targets positioned one hundred yards away.

The preparation for the Long Hike was brutal in itself. For weeks prior to the hike, we went on several shorter marches, all of which took place during the heat of the day. First we marched five miles, then ten miles, then two fifteens close together; and finally after a week's break, the Long Hike.

I will never forget my first one. Every Green Beret who had already experienced the Hike spoke of it in a way that evoked great apprehension among the rest of us.

We heard some terrifying stories...soldiers fainting mid-way in the middle of nowhere, others running out of water and dehydrating, guys getting hernias and suffering for the rest of their lives, backs going out, cramps setting in, people crying for their mommas…we even heard of a fatality that had occurred during the Long Hike years before.

Needless to say, my young comrades and I were very concerned.

The night of my first Hike, a few older, hardened soldiers sat down with some of us younger guys, and they talked to us like friends (a great rarity, because older soldiers were normally harsh and condescending towards recruits.)

We were stunned! That was the first time the seasoned warriors had been kind to us. They looked us in the eyes and spoke with care.

"What you are about to do is impossible. All the stories you heard are true. There is a point where you feel like your legs are going to fall off."

Ears perked….

"Well, we want to share with you what the older soldiers told us when we had to go through it the first time. May these words remain with you and help you through it."

We expected a long speech. We thought they would give us a lecture with pointers about what to do and not to do during the Hike. Surprisingly their advice comprised of just two sentences:

"It's all about the first step. If you take the first step boldly, you will be able to complete the Hike."

It was about eight o'clock in the evening when we all lined up single-file in a large field. The mood was very somber. No one was speaking. Everyone knew what was expected of him. Even the officers in charge had little to say.

The commander of our Green Beret unit climbed to the highest point of a stone wall and with his booming voice he ordered,

"Forwaaaaaard......."

My mind was on overload.

It's all about the first step, Marios. First step...the first step. Just take the first step...and take that first step boldly.

"...Maaarch!"

I took a giant step forward, bringing the back of my heel forcefully into the dirt for emphasis. One hundred other Green Berets did likewise. "Khhhhhhh" went our heels, and off we were to conquer that night's impossibility.

The sound of that first step will ring in my ears for life.

I completed the Long Hike just fine that night. In fact, there were four of them on my record before my conscription ended.

What our older comrades shared with us the night before our first Long Hike is true, especially for the believer in Jesus Christ. The first step puts faith into action and proves to us, to God, and to the kingdom of darkness, that we are determined to move forward with confidence.

Most great things we accomplish in life don't start out to be promising. They start out as forbidden realms, places where there are huge signs posted up saying,

"Impossible! Keep Out! No Trespassing! It's not for you, not right now, not ever. You can't do this!"

The moment we enter into seemingly forbidden realms and see the "Stay Away!" signs, instead of heeding the signs and turning back, we must press beyond what we see in the natural. By faith, we must access God's supernatural love and power, and then boldly take the first step towards the impossible.

May the Lord Jesus grant you courage and strength to take *your* first step towards life's "long hikes." May He help you take that step boldly; and may He encourage, direct, love, and protect you the rest of the way!

God is with us! Join me in running towards the impossible!

For More Information Contact:

Marios Ellinas
Valley Shore Assembly of God
36 Great Hammock Road
Old Saybrook, CT 06475

Email: maellinas@yahoo.com

To order more copies of this book visit:

- Runningtotheimpossible.com

2/13/09, God TV, Denton, TX,
Messianic Jews
        align with
        who are apostle
        leaders in Israel
Your in authority: to give life
You are under author to receive life
        It's cyclical

Apostle Peter Wagner - Int'l Coalition
    "   Jay Swallow   of Apostles

chuck Pierce
Don & Patti Juster